The *Pawfect* Guide to Thinking Like a Dog

The *Pawfect* Guide to Thinking Like a Dog

Emma Milne and Karen Wild

THUNDER BAY
P·R·E·S·S
San Diego, California

Thunder Bay Press
An imprint of Printers Row Publishing Group
10350 Barnes Canyon Road, Suite 100, San Diego, CA 92121
www.thunderbaybooks.com

Project Editor: Sarah Uttridge
Design: Andrew Easton

Thunder Bay Press
Publisher: Peter Norton
Associate Publisher: Ana Parker
Publishing/Editorial Team: April Farr, Kelly Larsen, Kathryn C. Dalby
Editorial Team: JoAnn Padgett, Melinda Allman, Traci Douglas

Library of Congress Cataloging-in-Publication data is available upon request.

ISBN: 978-1-68412-286-8

Printed in China

22 21 20 19 18   1 2 3 4 5

CONTENTS

INTRODUCTION

Dogs are such incredible companions, well suited, even created, for living alongside humans. The very least we can do for them is to ensure their happiness. Our dogs need a lot of our care, time, attention, and sometimes money for their continued well-being. These 501 tips are intended to give you and your dog the "pawfect" way to live together as two different species merged for friendship and mutual benefit.

This handy guide takes you through every stage of dog ownership, from deciding whether to get a dog to raising your puppy or rescue dog and through your dog's adulthood into old age. The needs of dogs, and their behavioral and physical health, are the primary focus.

To use this guide, select a section, and study it to learn how best to treat your companion, both for physical and behavioral health. Dogs everywhere benefit from this updated knowledge, and now yours can as well, once you've read these 501 essential pieces of advice.

Dog ownership has pitfalls. Poor advice, superstitions, and outdated and painful training methods are rife in the dog world. Many breeding practices have not followed health and welfare recommendations. Extremes of body and head shape have been upheld as desirable traits in dogs, but these features can also cause exceptional suffering in the animals. This book describes the best ways to avoid such problems, which all dog owners stumble across. It also gives you confidence that your dog will have the healthiest life possible.

Should your dog experience problems during his or her lifespan, this book is here to support you, but you should also check with a vet if you have any concerns. The small, bite-size chunks of information are easy to digest and put into practice, too. Behavioral problems can be complicated, but this guide gives you the basics to help you get on a path to raising a much happier dog, and to being a happier you, too.

Let's get started! Sit down comfortably and begin learning about the exciting life you and your dog can enjoy together, thanks to these 501 fantastic tips!

BEFORE GETTING A DOG

1. RESEARCH

Knowing the five welfare needs of animals (food, environment, health, sociability, and behavior) is an excellent and simple way to think about the care of any animal, including dogs. Before getting any animals, you should research their needs and decide honestly if you can meet them.

2. NEEDS

Three of the five needs are physical things, such as a suitable place to live, and these are usually easiest to get right. The other two can be thought of as the happiness needs, and this is where many people go wrong, by not understanding an animal's full requirements.
The five welfare needs follow:

3. THE FIVE WELFARE NEEDS #1: FOOD

The need for the right food and water: Dogs are omnivores and eat both meat and plants, as most humans do. However, many human foods are poisonous to dogs, so always feed dog food to dogs. Fresh water should always be available as well.

4. THE FIVE WELFARE NEEDS #2: ENVIRONMENT

The need for the right environment: This will be an owner's home and yard or nearby areas, such as parks. You'll also need somewhere comfortable for your dog to sleep. Think carefully if you don't have access to an outdoor area where your dog can relieve itself; you'll have to take the dog for a walk when it needs to go.

5. THE FIVE WELFARE NEEDS #3: HEALTH

The need to be protected from pain, injury, and disease: Vaccinations, deworming, flea treatment, neutering, illnesses, and injuries cost a lot of money. Be realistic about the cost when you're thinking about pets. Dogs can cost up to $40,000 (£30,000) in a lifetime; the average is $18,615! (£14,000)

6. THE FIVE WELFARE NEEDS #4: SOCIABILITY

A dog is a social animal and can find being alone very frightening and frustrating. A dog is happy with canine or human company, but don't leave your dog alone for long periods of time.

7. THE FIVE WELFARE NEEDS #5: BEHAVIOR

The need to behave normally: A dog needs stimulation and exercise. There are millions of dogs that never get walked and even more that never get off their leads. This isn't fair. Walking, training, and playing with your dog are stimulating for you, too, so get out there and have some fun together!

8. HONESTY

If you already have a dog, think about these five needs, and ask yourself if there's any way you could do better. It's always good to keep challenging yourself. If you're thinking about getting a dog, research all these needs really well, and be HONEST with yourself!

9. PRACTICE

It's not okay to deprive a dog of one of its needs because it's inconvenient. A great tip before getting a dog is to go for a half-hour walk twice a day EVERY day for a month. It's harder than you think, especially in winter! If you pick an energetic breed, you'll need to go outside even more often than that.

10. LOVE

Accept that dogs drool, bark, whine, shed hair, get covered in mud, roll in gross things, eat gross things, and take time and energy. If you do accept these things, you'll find that dogs are the most wonderful companions humans could ever wish for.

11. ANCESTRY

Dogs are often compared with wolves, but their ancestry is misinterpreted. Both dogs and modern-day wolves are thought to have originated from a long-extinct prehistoric wolf-like ancestor, but the two groups split around 9,000 to 16,000 years ago. There are differences in how these species live and behave.

12. BREED HISTORY

Not all dog breeds originated from the same location. Studies suggest that Asiatic breeds, such as the chow chow and Akita, evolved separately from European dog breeds. Today's husky has been indicated to have a direct DNA link to an ancestor 35,000 years before.

13. DOMESTICATION

This is the way a species is trained or bred to live alongside and work with humans. Dogs are thought to have adapted to our specific living environments long ago, but mixed evidence means that the date at which their domestication began is uncertain. It is estimated to have happened from 11,000 to 32,000 years ago.

14. HOW DOGS LIVED WITH HUMANS

Once bred for food and fur, the dog's unique qualities of protectiveness, scent sensitivity, and hunting ability kept the species close to human homesteads. The dog's companionable nature appears to be a key quality that led to its living compatibly with human families.

15. DOGS IN HISTORY

Even in ancient times, dogs were granted access to our homes, sharing shelter and resources. Ancient dogs were bred for tasks such as pulling carts and working sheep, based on their geographical location. Some dogs were trained to perform and provide fun, as well as to behave as pets.

16. EARLY LEARNING

Dogs learn from everything around them, even when very young. If puppies are not handled during the neonatal stage, or even if their mothers are not petted during pregnancy, the lack of contact may impact the puppies' reactions later in life. The gentle handling offered while puppies are alert helps them learn not to fear human interaction.

17. INSTINCTIVE RESPONSES

These "knee-jerk" reactions are not learned; they are instant responses to stimuli. For example, a sudden movement toward your face might make you blink. Such a response is "unconditioned," meaning it is not taught. Instinctive responses such as this are used in dog training.

18. LINKING STIMULUS TO RESPONSE

In the late 1800s, Pavlov realized that dogs salivated at food's aroma. He developed a salivation response in dogs upon hearing a metronome by linking the occasion of food to the sound. Skinner then studied operant conditioning, linking cues or commands to learned behaviors.

19. CONDITIONED OR LEARNED RESPONSES

The science of behavior and conditioning extends to many everyday examples of how a dog learns. A dog that is scared by the loud bangs and whistles of fireworks may associate darkness with that same fear, subsequently becoming afraid of nighttime.

20. LEARNING WITH A PURPOSE

Dogs learn based on what is important to them, what benefits them, or what causes them to be unhappy. This affects every aspect of the dogs' lives.

21. SURROUNDINGS

Dogs are continually learning from their environment. The context of events affects their behavior, and the consequences of that behavior influence what they choose next.

22. CONSEQUENCES. GOOD OR BAD?

The outcomes of choices can be reinforcing, meaning rewarding, or punishing. Dogs may run, chase, or hunt and find or lose food, shelter, safety, or sexual partners. While dogs seek to fulfill their needs with their behaviors, they will have differing preferences.

23. TRAINING

Manipulating learning through training teaches dogs to work alongside humans. Normally, dogs will avoid punishment and seek reward. But punishment creates enormous stress in dogs and is not a suitable training method. Reward-based methods are effective, kind, and preferable.

24. WHAT DO DOGS FIND REWARDING?

This varies from dog to dog, and by what the dog is looking to achieve. Usually, strongly scented food attracts a dog's sense of smell, but other reinforcement, such as toys, can be used. The dog attempts to earn rewards by behaving in ways directed by the trainer.

25. WHAT DO DOGS FIND PUNISHING?

By definition, punishment causes a dog to do less of something or to entirely stop some behavior. Punishment can range from withholding something the dog wants until a behavior ceases to holding the lead tightly, shouting at the dog, or yanking the leash. These actions cause fear and trauma in a dog and are not suitable methods for training.

26. LINKING LEARNING CHAINS

As with all learning, a dog links events together and can use the links to predict outcomes. There is usually more than one behavior, known as a chain of behaviors, leading to a predicted outcome. Behavior chains can be very complex based on a dog's previous learning.

27. BEHAVIORIST

A behaviorist analyzes these learned behaviors in order to modify problem behaviors. Always employ a properly registered animal behaviorist.

28. EXPRESSION

Dogs may not use words to express their feelings, but their bodies show the state of their emotions. They may also vocalize. Their body signals communicate intent and help humans to understand them.

29. TAIL WAG

A dog's tail communicates the level of excitement reached. Research has shown that a dog's tail wags more to the right when seeing a familiar person. It wags more to the left when the dog is with unfamiliar or worrying people. A dog isn't simply happy if it's wagging its tail.

30. EYE MOVEMENTS

A dog will look away when feeling a little overwhelmed. The dog's eyes may stare hard when agitated or about to lunge or chase. The eyes can appear soft when the dog is in a happy, relaxed state.

31. EAR MOVEMENTS

Dogs use their ears to orient toward sound. Their ears move back against their heads when they feel under pressure or fearful. Dogs will also move their ears back when greeting a favored human. Examine this and other body signals to check if all is well.

32. MOUTH SIGNALS

A dog that is experiencing increasing stress will yawn and lick its lips. It begins to hold its mouth more tightly as tension increases. An unhappy dog will seem to grin, pulling the corners of the closed mouth back. A relaxed dog holds the mouth open, often with the tongue lolling.

33. HEAD MOVEMENTS

Dogs with short fur may display wrinkling of their foreheads as they become alert. Their heads will orient toward targets that are of interest to them.

34. LEAVE ME ALONE!

Dogs under stress will turn their heads or whole bodies away, avoiding contact. This is a sign that the dogs wish to be left in peace.

35. BODY SIGNALS

These signals should not be read in isolation. A dog experiences conflicting emotions when unsure. The signals can be hard to interpret. Look for the level of your dog's arousal. If you see tension, call your dog to you and have the dog sit in order to calm down.

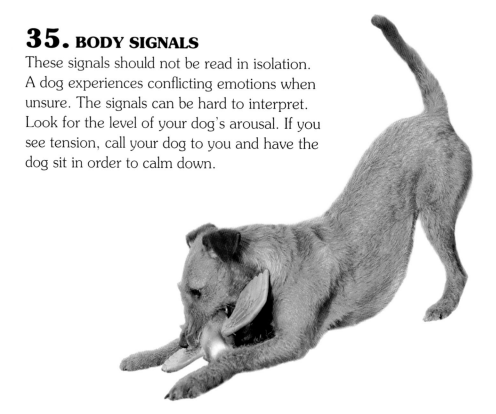

36. THE LANGUAGE OF PLAY

When dogs play, their body language includes signals that invite others to join in. Their paws slap to the ground, and they lower the front of their bodies, doing a "play bow" with their rears in the air. They prance back and forth.

37. CHASE ME!

A playful dog will perform a short run away from another dog to encourage a chase, with soft eyes and an open, panting mouth.

38. THE LANGUAGE OF FEAR

When a dog is fearful, its body is tense and stiff. The dog will stare or attempt to turn away. If a dog's body language is very stiff and still, immediately try to distract or call the dog away, so that a conflict does not escalate.

39. BREED AND PEDIGREE

All dogs are *Canis familiaris*, the same species. Yet, various dogs are placed in human-made categories called breeds, based on groups of similar-looking dogs found living worldwide. The breeds differ in their appearances. Their ancestry is tracked by what is known as a pedigree.

40. BREED FUNCTION

Humans established each breed's functions through artificial selection that aimed to maintain certain characteristics in the dogs. Put simply, a dog that was good for hunting would be matched with another, in the hope that the resulting puppies would inherit such ability. Behaviors such as hunting ability would be established in a breed when deemed useful for humans.

41. BREED FORM

A dog's intended job affected its ultimate form and shape. A sleek sighthound would be bred for its speed as a hunter. A short-legged dog would be designed to dig out vermin. Each breed's physical characteristics were intended for practical purposes, but now such intentions tend to be replaced by preferences for how a dog looks, or fashionable choices.

42. BREED STANDARDS

The standards are guidelines describing the characteristics, temperament, and appearance for a breed, intended to ensure that the breed is fit for its function. Size measurements, posture, tail carriage, and coat color are listed. Over the years, such characteristics have changed, and some standards are no longer fitting for ideal health or temperament.

43. A PET DOG BREED

Given that there are millions of dog owners in the world, dogs that once were bred for work purposes are now being used as pets, when this may not suit the dogs' or owners' needs. The job of being dog owners often comprises meeting the needs of dogs made for working.

44. NATURE OR NURTURE?

Every dog is a product of what is learned throughout their lifetimes, plus the characteristics they have inherited. It can be hard to predict how puppies will develop, since they are learning from every moment. Even a litter of puppies that look similar can have individuals that behave and develop very differently.

45. ADAPTABILITY

Dogs are highly adaptable as a species, but some have powerful instincts or physiques that, in the wrong home, can lead to serious maladaptive behaviors.

46. LEARNING

An older dog has learned a great deal over time, and simply hoping your puppy will turn out the same way is unrealistic. Read about the ways to treat your dog well. You're already doing that here, so well done!

47. LIFE STAGES

Your dog's behavior may change as the dog ages, so don't assume that your energetic adolescent will always be the same!

48. USING BREED TO PREDICT BEHAVIOR

It's a mistake to assume that just because one dog you met of a particular breed behaved in ways you enjoyed means that another of the same breed or similar looks will act the same way. Yet there is some evidence to suggest that undesirable breed traits, such as fearful behaviors, can be inherited.

49. GENES

Pedigree animals are inbred to keep them all looking the same as the breed. This means that the gene pool is relatively small, and in some breeds, very small indeed. This, in turn, means that unhealthy genes can be multiplied among them. Many of these breeds tend to suffer certain diseases. Of course, not all pedigree dogs have problems, but you need to be aware of the worst affected.

50. INHERITED DISEASE

Some breeds have much higher levels of inherited disease than others, and it's really important to speak to a vet and do extra research before getting a certain breed. You need to know how likely the dog is to get ill and decide if you think it's fair to buy a dog knowing it will probably suffer from a problem.

51. HEART DISEASE

This is very common in giant dogs such as Great Danes and also in other breeds such as Dobermans, boxers, and Cavalier King Charles spaniels. Heart disease is one of the biggest causes of young death in giant dogs and can be very expensive to treat, especially in large breeds.

52. JOINTS

Many large breeds are prone to joint and growth problems. Hip and elbow dysplasia is common in Labradors, retrievers, and German shepherds, but many breeds can be affected.

53. SKIN

Skin allergies and skin disease are more common in some breeds. Skin problems can be horrible for both your pet and you, and these are often lifelong issues. Breeds commonly affected are West Highland terriers, boxers, Labradors, bulldogs, basset hounds, and Shar-Peis.

54. CANCER

Cancer affects many older animals, but some breeds are prone to cancer more than others. Rottweilers, German shepherds, and flat-coated retrievers are some of the breeds more likely to get tumors, but remember to research any breed.

55. SHAPES

Dogs come in many shapes and sizes, and by selective breeding humans have created many dogs in shapes not found in nature. Sadly, some of the extremes of body shape also cause suffering in the dogs, so think carefully about natural dog shapes when picking from certain breeds.

56. SHORT LEGS

Dogs with very short legs have chondrodystrophy, a bit like dwarfism. This can affect their movement and also cause early arthritis because the bones are twisted and the joints don't align properly. In combination with a long back, it can be even more of a problem.

57. LONG BACKS

Dogs with long backs and short legs are much more likely to have spinal problems. The short legs go hand in hand with cartilage problems, and this affects the discs in the spine, too. A long back is like a weak, unsupported bridge, and eventually the backs of these dogs can collapse. Some dogs with long backs may do well with surgery, but some become paralyzed.

58. SKIN FOLDS

People seem to think wrinkles are cute on animals. For dogs, having many wrinkles can cause problems. Skin is usually perfectly balanced, but folds trap moisture, lose their air supply, and become inflamed. The skin gets damaged, and bacteria get in so the folds are often painfully and chronically infected.

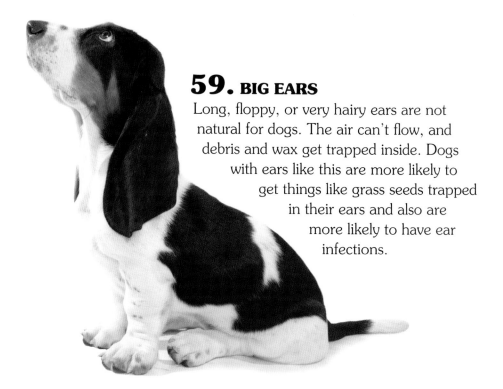

59. BIG EARS

Long, floppy, or very hairy ears are not natural for dogs. The air can't flow, and debris and wax get trapped inside. Dogs with ears like this are more likely to get things like grass seeds trapped in their ears and also are more likely to have ear infections.

60. BALD DOGS

Hairless or partially hairless dogs are more prone to injury, cold, and sunburn and are best avoided.

61. GIANT BREEDS

Giant breeds tend to have the shortest lifespans because of things like heart disease, cancer, and joint problems. You may not have issues, or you may only have your big dog for four to six years, in some cases. You also need to remember that drugs cost more for each pound or kilo the animal weighs, so these guys can be very expensive to treat.

62. TEACUPS

Tiny little teacup dogs are very popular at the moment. People have produced them by picking the smallest of litters, often the runts, and breeding them. These dogs are extremely fragile and very prone to health problems.

63. SHORT FACES

Short-faced dogs like bulldogs, French bulldogs, and pugs are very popular and considered cute. In fact, these dogs suffer the worst effects of body shape. Many can't breathe properly and struggle their whole lives. They have a hard time staying cool, and are very prone to heat exhaustion. Their bulging eyes are more likely to get injured, so many lose an eye from trauma. These breeds often suffer with deformed vertebrae and spinal problems.

64. HEALTH TESTS

There are lots of health tests for animals, so make sure you find out all that you can about your chosen breed and what health tests are available. This will also help when it comes to picking a breeder or adopting a rescue dog.

65. DESIGNER CROSSBREEDS

These are also popular these days and include breeds such as Labradoodles, cockapoos, cavapoos, and all manner of others. Some of these animals will be okay, but some will end up with the health issues of both parent breeds, so be very careful if you're thinking of one of these.

66. MONGRELS

Consider a good old mongrel. True crossbreeds or mongrels are less likely to have health issues than pedigreed dogs, and are usually a good bet. Whatever you do, try to remember Mother Nature, and pick a dog that is proportioned and shaped as a dog should be!

67. BREED TYPES

It's easy to identify different breeds of dog, but most people choose their breeds on looks alone. This is a bad idea. Many dogs have attractive appearances but are utterly unsuited to family lifestyles. Others have bad reputations that are undeserved. Crossbreeds provide an even greater variety of characteristics.

68. LARGE BREEDS

Larger dogs are naturally more powerful and take up a great deal of space and resources. Food, insurance costs, and medical costs are all higher with a larger dog.

69. SMALLER BREEDS

Smaller dogs may be physically easier to manage but still need considerable care. Some small breeds are highly energetic and muscular, so they take increased time and energy.

70. ENERGETIC AND WORKING BREEDS

Any breed described as "working," or any famed for the jobs they do, such as herding, guarding flocks, following scents, pulling sleds, or doing gundog work, will need a great deal of space and exercise. It is not enough to walk them twice a day and then leave them alone. They need high levels of attention and stimulation.

71. LAPDOGS

Bear in mind that dogs were traditionally bred for the job they
had to do. Companionship traits are often more prevalent in dogs
traditionally bred for sitting indoors and being petted. This is not to
say that larger dogs cannot have these traits, but choose a dog for the
purpose you intend for it.

72. BREED BEHAVIOR PROBLEMS

It is difficult to identify specific
breeds that are likely to have
temperament or behavior
problems. These issues are
most likely to arise with owners
that have chosen breed and
temperament types that are
incompatible with their lifestyles.

73. RESEARCH YOUR BREED

Do thorough research, and listen to experts who tell you that your choice of dog may not suit you. All dogs are beautiful, and a breeder often wants to make a sale, but those with integrity will sell only to suitable owners.

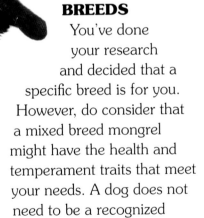

74. GOOD OR BAD BREEDS?

There is no such thing as an ideal breed. Look for health, temperament, and lifestyle compatibility.

75. MIXED BREEDS

You've done your research and decided that a specific breed is for you. However, do consider that a mixed breed mongrel might have the health and temperament traits that meet your needs. A dog does not need to be a recognized crossbreed.

76. ADOPTION

Before you think about a breeder, always consider adoption. You may think you'll never find what you're looking for in an adoption center because you're certain of what you want. BUT what harm can it do? There's no obligation to take any dog home, and you might just fall in love.

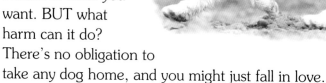

77. CIRCUMSTANCES

Sadly, there are thousands of dogs all over the world that have been given up through no fault of their own. People get divorced, owners die, jobs get lost, and financial situations change. Don't assume that all animals in need of a home are "problem children." If you really want a puppy, you can usually put your name on a waiting list.

78. GOLDEN OLDIES

Sometimes, adopting older animals can have lots of bonuses, too. You avoid the chewing phase and housetraining! Depending on the age of dog you take on, you could also get a well-trained or more sedate dog that might not need quite so much energy to look after.

79. MATCHMAKING

Most good adoption centers are excellent at matching animals to your circumstances. So many animals are rehomed because of the bad choices their owners made in the first place. By getting advice from an adoption center, you can be more certain of a great match for you and your family.

80. GOOD CAUSES

By adopting, you are contributing to a great cause and also immediately improving the life of one animal, which goes from a cage to the comfort of a loving home. Most centers also offer ongoing help with behavior and health advice, too.

81. JUST FOR US

Before you call or message
that breeder you found on the
internet, promise one thing—that
you'll spend a couple of hours
wandering the aisles of your
local adoption center. You
might be surprised.

82. PUPPY FARMS

If you find adoption really isn't right for you then picking the right
breeder is absolutely essential. All over the world, puppy farms and
mills are a massive problem, affecting the health and welfare of
dogs. Too many people don't spend enough time researching good
breeders, and too many potential owners fall
into the puppy farm traps.

83. ISOLATION

Breeding dogs on puppy farms live isolated lives, usually in horrible, squalid, and filthy conditions. Their nutrition is poor, and the hygiene is almost nonexistent. They seldom or never get affection or exercise and are used like machines, producing litter after litter.

84. WEAK PUPPIES

Puppies that come from puppy farms very often spend their whole lives ill or even die at a young age. They have poor immunity, haven't been vaccinated or treated for worms, and often haven't had the right food or even clean water. Puppy farms are not good!

85. ILLEGAL IMPORTS

In many parts of the world, there is also a problem with illegally imported puppies. This is a big problem for the same reasons that puppy farms are, but it is also an issue because the puppies are moved at such young ages. Very young animals are more likely to die from dehydration on their journeys, and the risk of spreading diseases like rabies is much higher.

86. SYMPATHY

Lots of people realize that farm-raised puppies are sickly or malnourished, but sympathy keeps the demand going. People often feel like they need to save individual puppies. They take the animals on, but this perpetuates the problem and can be heartbreaking for the families involved.

87. MOMS!

NEVER buy a puppy without seeing its mother and where it was raised. If someone offers to meet you somewhere to hand over the puppy, do not accept this. This is often a front for a farm. If you go to a house, but there's an excuse why the mother isn't there, don't accept it and walk away. If a breeder is advertising lots of different breeds, the breeder is best avoided.

88. BE BOLD

Good breeders will have only a small number of dogs and will let the bitches have only a certain number of litters in their lives. Good breeders will do all the health tests available for their breed. Don't be afraid to ask questions, and expect answers. Health test results should be openly available.

89. WHERE DO I START?

The internet, breeding organizations, local advertisements, cards in pet stores, and sometimes neighbors may offer pups. However, convenience, price, or availability is never the first priority when choosing a breeder. The temperament and health of the dog top the list.

90. BREEDER CREDENTIALS

A good breeder usually has a lot of information about his or her dogs. Do a quick search online to reveal any mention of the breeder's reputation. If you can't find information, treat the situation with suspicion. Likewise, if the breeder has multiple breeds of dog available, this is likely to be a puppy mill. Avoid at all costs.

91. BREEDING BEHAVIOR PITFALLS

Puppies that are raised away from a home environment, in a kennel or shed, do not adapt well to human family life. There is an early and critical socialization period for pups, when they must be raised around people, children, and households. Without this, the puppies develop long-term fear issues as well as hyper-reactivity to the world around them.

92. QUESTIONS TO ASK: SOCIAL CONTACT

Have the puppies been mixing with children and visitors? If they have, how often, and for how long? Puppies must be around household noises such as refrigerators, banging doors, and other family hubbub. Puppies must meet lots of people in order to socialize.

93. QUESTIONS TO ASK: REARING

How does the mother behave around her puppies? If the mother is defensive, it's likely her pups will inherit this characteristic. Some breeding mothers are relaxed and confident, which are preferable traits.

94. QUESTIONS TO ASK: HOUSE-TRAINING

Where do the puppies relieve themselves? Is there a specific area? Puppies allowed to defecate anywhere will create havoc when you attempt to house-train them.

95. A GREAT BREEDER

A good breeder will ask more questions than you ask. Never be upset if a breeder tells you that you are not right for his or her pups. A good breeder should be concerned for the dogs' welfare more than yours.

96. CONSUMER RIGHTS

A good breeder has an official puppy contract, which details all the tests the puppies have had, as well as vaccinations and other puppy routines. It will give the breeder first right to return if there is a problem. Your breeder should observe the legal trading laws in your country.

97. BE READY TO WALK AWAY

Never, ever take a puppy home out of sympathy if the breeder doesn't appear suitable. You are only making room for another suffering puppy. Quality breeders can be hard to find, so be patient and do plenty of research.

98. FEEDING QUESTIONS

Are the puppies fed in separate bowls? Pups that have been feeding from the same bowl may develop resource-guarding issues. This is because the puppies have to fight for any food available to them. This teaches them to engage in defensive behaviors at an early age.

PUPPIES!

99. BEHAVIORAL HEALTH

The health needs of dogs extend beyond the physical. Their mental health is dependent on social interaction and on being able to express themselves freely.

100. THE OWNER'S JOB

A dog's behavior is the responsibility of its owner, falling within legal requirements, such as keeping the dog on a leash. This can interfere with your pup's free expression of behavior. Positive reinforcement-based training allows the owner to control the dog within legal and social parameters, without inhibiting the dog's behavioral welfare.

101. MIXING

Social interaction with other dogs must be commenced as early as possible. Dogs meet other dogs on walks and in public spaces and must not feel alarmed. Attending puppy preschools and meeting vaccinated adult dogs will help puppies to learn the rules gently.

102. HUMAN FAMILIES

Dogs live in human families, meeting people at all stages of life. Puppies are best introduced to a wide range of humans, such as children and the elderly, as well as loud people, quiet people, and so on. Even physical features, such as wearing eyeglasses or not, can appear unusual to puppies and be scary if they are not familiar with these ways of appearing.

103. INSTINCTS

Foraging and scavenging are normal dog behaviors that allow a dog to engage its instincts. These behaviors can develop into problems if the dog chews or swallows items that are not suitable. With training, your dog can learn to sniff out interesting items on cue, and be distracted from those things that may cause harm.

104. BE KIND

Training methods such as punishment and shock collars are strongly linked to behavioral problems, either creating or escalating adverse emotional reactions. Animals have a right to live free from pain and fear. Smacking, shouting, or using an electric shock in attempts to train animals create negative responses and are outdated and unnecessary.

105. HEARING

A dog's hearing sensitivity can create noise phobias, where the dog is startled by sudden or loud sounds. Noise can even be painful. A dog must become used to everyday noises, which may be unsettling at first. Preparations should be made to relax and protect your dog during firework season.

106. SCENT

This is a dog's primary sense, but it can lead a dog astray if a tempting scent appears. If there is a female in heat nearby, this can lead to barking and frustration in some male dogs. A dog interprets scent in great detail, leaving the humans uncertain why the animal is reacting when nothing visible is apparent.

107. HEALTHY WALKS

The walks a dog takes should allow him or her to perform important behaviors, such as foraging and exploration, scenting the environment, using personal scent markers, and enjoying companionship with other dogs and humans.

108. NOT ENOUGH EXERCISE

The 2016 PDSA Animal Wellbeing (PAW) Report indicated that very few dogs actually get regularly exercised. Every dog needs a walk at least twice a day. A tired dog is a well-behaved dog!

109. TRAIN PUPPIES

A puppy rarely grows out of early behaviors. Redirecting and training a young dog, using positive reinforcement methods, reduces the risk of the development of behavioral issues. Start at the earliest opportunity, as your dog will always learn something, whether or not it is useful learning.

110. PICK ME!

So you've found a breeder you're happy with, and now it's time to pick your actual puppy. You can just ask the breeder to pick one for you out of the melee, but it's worth going to see the litter as soon as the breeder will allow it to make sure you're happy. This dog will hopefully be part of your family for around fifteen years, so you need to be sure!

111. IS SHE THE MOTHER?

When you go to the house, look for signs that the mother is actually the mother. Puppy dealers sometimes pretend. Has she bonded with the puppies? Does she have swollen mammary glands?

112. MALE OR FEMALE?

You may well already have a very clear idea about which sex to pick, or you may not be bothered. Some diseases are more common in males, and others in females, but there are other things to consider. Neutering a female is more expensive and involves more surgery than taking care of a male. Also consider the possible behavioral differences covered in our behavior section.

113. HYGIENE

When you go to see your puppy, the house should be clean and welcoming. Good hygiene is very important. Try to get a feel for the health of the mother as well as the litter. Do they all look well fed and have shiny coats?

114. FOOD AND WATER

Can you see food and clean water available? Even if the puppies are too young to have food yet, all nursing mothers should have access to good-quality puppy food at all times. This is so they can meet the energy needs of feeding their brood.

115. VISITS

Breeders should be happy for you to visit as many times as you want to, within reason. Don't get bullied into handing over your money and taking the puppy that day. Be suspicious if they do this. It may be a sign of a puppy farm.

116. PREVENTATIVE HEALTH

Good breeders should be open about the vaccine and worm treatments they use for both the mother and the puppies, and show you certificates if the puppy is old enough to have had its first vaccine. Make sure you ask.

117. PUPPY HEALTH CHECKS

There are certain things you should look for in a puppy that are signs of good health, besides being well nourished. Check these things each time you visit your puppy to make sure they are consistently good:

118. PUPPY HEALTH CHECKS #1: MOVEMENT

Your puppy should be moving around normally, with no signs of lameness or other issues. If your puppy is asleep every time you go, this could be a sign of ill health. If the breeder always hands you the puppy to hold, put your puppy down so you can see how it moves.

119. PUPPY HEALTH CHECKS #2: EYES

Your puppy should have bright, clear eyes unless it is still tiny and the eyes are still shut. If there is a lot of discharge or if the eyes are red or swollen, do not take the puppy. Make sure the eyelids are not rolled in on the surface of the eye or drooping down.

120. PUPPY HEALTH CHECKS #3: NOSE

Not all noses are wet and shiny, but it's a good sign if they are. Look out for sneezing or mucus, as these could be signs of problems or of a generally weak puppy.

121. PUPPY HEALTH CHECKS #4: EARS

Ears should be clean and not smelly. Head shaking, scratching, and signs of wax or debris in the ears could indicate ear mites or infections.

122. PUPPY HEALTH CHECKS #5: COAT

The fur should be clean and shiny. Look out for scabs, black dots that could be a sign of fleas, and bald patches. Frequent scratching could also be a sign of problems.

123. PUPPY HEALTH CHECKS #6: BOTTOMS!

Your puppy's bottom should be clean and free of poop. If it's dirty, this could be a sign of diarrhea or of a sickly mother that isn't cleaning her puppies properly.

124. PUPPY HEALTH CHECKS #7: BREATHING

Your puppy should be breathing silently and with no signs of labored breathing. If you hear snoring, snorting, or wheezing, do not take that puppy. It's not normal!

125. CONTRACTS

Look into puppy contracts in your country. Any breeders who won't sign contracts to say they've done all they can for the health of the puppies should be avoided.

126. PUPPY INFORMATION

Look out for online puppy information packs and guidance notes that help arm you with all the questions you should ask your breeder. Make sure you stay in charge of your decisions.

127. NEW HOME

Bringing a new puppy into your family is a huge responsibility. It is very easy to find puppies for sale, but quality well-bred puppies with good health and essential early socialization are hard to find. Prepare to spend several months searching for a good-quality puppy.

128. ADVERTISING

Online advertisements will always show attractive photos of cute puppies. The images do not show the reality of puppy farming or the kind of poor care that affects puppy behavior. Puppies must be raised in a home environment if they are to settle into one.

129. SEE THE FAMILY!

Ask to see the puppy with its mother. This helps you to meet her and see how she behaves. A good breeder will proudly show you the father dog, older siblings, and other relatives. This is the best way to work out how your puppy will be.

130. CHOICE OF PUP

Aim to see the whole litter at least three times before choosing. This gives you the chance to see the pups when they are alert as well as tired. Look for play. Do the pups interact with each other and with people?

131. PUPPY TYPE

Ask the breeder to tell you about the pups, as he or she should want the puppy to have a good, suitable home. Avoid the extremes of behavior, for example a very quiet puppy or a very boisterous one. Try to pick one that has a bit of each quality.

132. ASSESSMENT

Take each puppy into a separate room and see how it behaves. If the puppy panics, this might not be a good sign. If the puppy shows no signs of worry and mouths you hard, again, this may not be desirable. Look for a puppy whose behavior you feel comfortable with.

133. TWO PUPS?

Avoid the temptation to take two puppies at once. Experienced professional trainers advise against this. Young dogs take a lot of work and time to help them learn how to behave in a human setting. This becomes even harder as they reach adolescence.

134. EXTRA PROBLEMS

Taking two puppies at once prevents thorough training and socialization. They often bond strongly without letting humans into the relationship. This creates problems with separation distress and control. Each dog needs separate training, no matter what the circumstances are.

135. OLDER DOGS

Aim to choose a puppy that will be compatible with your older dog, if you have one. If your older dog is in pain or otherwise feeling poorly, he or she will not appreciate a young, exuberant puppy. Ideally, consider that each dog will need its own space, own walks, and own feeding areas.

136. DON'T BUY

Be prepared to walk away from any litter you aren't comfortable with. This takes a lot of strength. However, it is rarely possible to fix a puppy that has been poorly bred and poorly socialized. You will have a dog for about 15 years, and that commitment means you should also spend your time choosing the one you really want.

137. PUPPY CHOICE

Avoid just taking the puppy that chooses you. This is likely to be the boldest puppy in the litter, and that dog may not suit your family.

Ignore coat colors and markings, and look instead for the puppy whose temperament you feel is most attractive to you.

138. WHERE IN THE WORLD?

Different countries have very different laws about what is considered a mutilation. Regardless of the laws, chopping bits off dogs because some people think they look better like that is unnecessary and cruel. Leave your dogs as nature intended!

139. DEW CLAWS

Dogs can have dew claws on their front and back legs. On the hind legs, these claws are sometimes very floppy and not firmly attached—the back ones have no use and not all dogs have them. Some people ask for them to be removed at birth or at neutering.

140. DOGGY THUMBS!

When you watch dogs chewing toys or food chews, they use their front dew claws, a bit like we use our thumbs, to help hold things. The dew claws occasionally get snagged, but this can be dealt with when that happens. The claws don't need to be removed ahead of time just in case!

141. EAR CROPPING

This is illegal in many countries but definitely still goes on in lots of places. People think cropped ears make dogs look tougher. Ear cropping is an unnecessary mutilation and should never be done.

142. TAIL DOCKING

This is where part or all of the puppy's tail is cut off within a few days of birth or has an elastic band put on until it falls off. Tail docking is very painful and almost always done with no anesthetic.

143. BREED

Being a certain breed isn't an excuse to have a body part amputated for no reason. Just because some breeds are traditionally docked doesn't mean you have to accept that. Look for a breeder that doesn't dock tails.

144. COMMUNICATION

Dogs' tails are used for balance, but tails are also really important for communicating with other dogs. Docked animals sometimes draw aggression from other dogs and frighten people because their mood is unclear.

145. PREVENTING INJURY

This is a poor argument for tail docking. Any dogs can occasionally hurt their tails, and some will need their tails amputated in later life. BUT docking injures EVERY dog in the worst way and is not justified.

146. COMPLICATIONS

Tail docking can cause phantom pain, painful neuromas where the nerves have been cut, spinal infections, and poor growth for a time afterward. Some puppies will bleed to death.

147. SPEAK IN ADVANCE

Because docking is done when the puppies are so very young, you will need to tell your breeder beforehand if you want your puppy to keep this very important part of its body. Preferably, don't choose a breeder who docks in the first place!

148. PUPPY DEVELOPMENT STAGES

There are stages that mark developmental levels, but these vary from one puppy to the next. The stages are described in time-sensitive periods that may overlap rather than be clearly defined. A puppy's experience during these stages can form its responses in adult life.

149. PUPPY DEVELOPMENT STAGES #1: PRENATAL (BEFORE BIRTH)

Before birth, the mother's experiences of stress or other conditions may influence the unborn puppy.

150. PUPPY DEVELOPMENT STAGES #2: NEONATAL (BIRTH TO 2 WEEKS)

At this stage, the pups are completely dependent on their mother for food, warmth, and safety. The mother dog licks the pups to stimulate them to "go." Scent and touch help the pups to learn, and they seek to suckle for food.

151. PUPPY DEVELOPMENT STAGES #3: TRANSITIONAL (2 TO 3 WEEKS)

Pups begin to stand and walk, a little shakily at first, but can gradually start to pass water and defecate independently, away from the nest. Puppies begin to play with their siblings, wag their tails, and may even growl!

152. PUPPY DEVELOPMENT STAGES #4: AT 18 TO 20 DAYS

The pup's ear canals and their eyes open, and the puppy startles at noises. The puppy moves around a lot more and will make vocalizations when separated from the mother.

153. PUPPY DEVELOPMENT STAGES #5: SOCIALIZATION (3 TO 13 WEEKS)

At this stage, the puppies learn a great deal about their world. Their behavioral development is at its most rapid, and they must experience a wide range of situations if they are to cope with the many challenges facing a pet dog.

154. PUPPY DEVELOPMENT STAGES #6: JUVENILE (13 WEEKS TO ADULT)

Having already begun to form social and emotional attachments, the puppy's strength and skills develop further. This period lasts until the pup reaches sexual maturity. Social maturity takes significantly longer to develop.

155. PUPPY DEVELOPMENT STAGES #7: ADULTHOOD (6 TO 18 MONTHS ONWARD)

This stage is highly dependent on breed. Adolescence can be a challenging time, as the growing puppy is still learning the rules of daily life while also appearing to be fully grown. Young dogs at the early stage of adulthood need careful guidance.

156. EARLY SOCIALIZATION

Taking care with this step prevents a
young puppy from fearing the world.
This care must begin as early as five
weeks of age, while the puppy is still
with its mother. Gentle handling while
the pup is alert and being reared in
a home help the pup to adjust to
the human world.

157. FAMILIAR AND UNFAMILIAR

Social contact must be established early, while the puppy is still
learning to tell the difference between familiar and safe situations and
unfamiliar or unsafe situations. The contact must vary a great deal, so
that the puppy can meet new experiences with confidence.

158. HABITUATION

This describes how pups get used to surroundings and learn that they are part of life, by becoming familiar with what happens in the background. For example, puppies learn to ignore the noise of the refrigerator or washing machine just by being around these machines.

159. SOCIALIZATION

This consists of multiple components. Puppies are exposed gently to many types of people, dogs, and other pets, such as cats or even livestock, so that they become familiar with these variations. Contact is restricted until the puppies are fully vaccinated.

160. OUTDOORS

The puppy should be encouraged to become used to traveling in the car, hearing and seeing other traffic, being in new places, and walking on new surfaces, such as gravel on a driveway or sand at a beach, once the young dog is fully vaccinated.

161. POSITIVE EXPERIENCES

When the puppy is around exciting, new situations, some parts of the experiences can be scary. Allow the pup time to explore, and offer comfort as well as small pieces of food, to increase feelings of safety and enjoyment. Keep sessions short and fun, giving the puppy time to rest.

162. TIMING OF SOCIALIZATION

The period during which puppies are most sensitive to learning of this kind is around 8 to 12 weeks of age. This critical period cannot be replaced, and it is crucial that the owner, or the breeder, takes responsibility for this social learning.

163. INFECTION RISK

Although a pup has not yet had its full vaccinations, socialization must not be delayed. Carry your puppy and ensure your companion is not in contact with unvaccinated dogs or other infection risks. Do not delay socialization, but simply observe and account for risks associated with disease.

164. FAILURE TO SOCIALIZE

Puppies that are not socialized can suffer severe problems in later life. Without socialization, hypersensitivity to new events, as well as fearful reactions, can create long-term stress. Remedial socialization is constantly required and cannot replace the early opportunity to learn.

165. MIXING WITH OTHER DOGS

Well-socialized pups have had the chance to play with dogs of all shapes, colors, and sizes. Puppies play together quite roughly, but adult dogs will teach new puppies the social rules of play without injuring them. This self-handicapping play means new pups are taught the rules gently but firmly.

166. CHILDREN ARE FUN!

Children can move quickly, can be loud and shrill, and can play roughly and hug and kiss puppies in ways an older dog might not tolerate. Just as puppies have to learn human rules through early social contact, children must learn how to be sensible around dogs, too.

167. VACCINATION

Vaccination in every species, including humans, is a hot topic of conversation. Over-vaccination is something we all need to be mindful of, but vaccines are essential in general. Vaccinations have saved millions of human and animal lives.

168. TAKE HEED

Don't be fooled by those who say that some diseases are not an issue anymore. Believe your vet. Seeing unvaccinated dogs die from preventable diseases is something every vet dreads. Work with your vet to create a vaccine plan for your pet.

169. GET A VET'S ADVICE

Where you live will dictate what vaccines your dog needs, so talk to your vet about what is necessary. The World Small Animal Veterinary Association (WSAVA) website has excellent information about the most up-to-date guidelines and safety, too —just go to the "Vaccinations, guidelines" section.

170. ESSENTIAL

Some vaccines are called core vaccines, and these are considered essential for all dogs, no matter where in the world you are. The three core vaccines for all dogs are for canine distemper, canine parvovirus, and infectious canine hepatitis. Many countries also require a rabies vaccination, as this is a deadly disease for humans as well as animals.

171. RABIES

Rabies is a huge cause of death, especially in developing countries. Rabies spreads when infected animals bite others. Dogs and bats most commonly spread the disease. Rabies attacks the brain and causes many signs of infection, including twitching, confusion, fear of water, and coma. It is almost always fatal.

172. DISTEMPER

Distemper is related to human measles and
can be fatal. In puppies, it has a death
rate of more than 50 percent. Signs of
the disease can range from coughing,
wheezing, twitching, seizures, vomiting,
diarrhea, and weight loss to death.
Many wild animals carry distemper, so
protection by vaccination is
very important.

173. PARVOVIRUS

Parvovirus is a horrible disease that readily kills pet dogs and wild
dogs. Untreated, most animals will die in a couple of days, and death
can still occur even with treatment. Parvovirus causes fever, severe
vomiting, and bloody diarrhea. Vaccination is essential.

174. HEPATITIS

Infectious hepatitis is another potentially deadly disease that causes fever, depression, liver disease, and kidney disease. Dogs often get a blue sheen to their eyes because of an immune reaction. This has led some people to call the disease "blue eye."

175. LOCATION

There are other important vaccines available, depending on your location. Just because the vaccines needed for your dog are not on the worldwide list doesn't mean that in some countries or in your area they aren't considered just as important. These vaccines fight illnesses such as leptospirosis, kennel cough, and borreliosis, or Lyme's disease.

176. TYPES

In general, there are two types of vaccine; infectious and noninfectious. The infectious ones tend to last longer and cause a bigger immune reaction because they have active viruses or bacteria in them that have been changed in the lab. Some noninfectious vaccines must be given yearly, while some infectious ones last for a number of years.

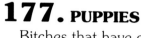

177. PUPPIES

Bitches that have good immunity to vaccinations will pass on a maternal immunity to their pups. This can stop vaccines from working, a result that varies a lot among individual puppies. That's why puppies receive two or more doses of vaccines to make sure all the puppies are protected against all the diseases.

178. SCHEDULE

Normally, puppies have their first vaccination at around eight to nine weeks of age, but this routine can start as young as six weeks, in some instances. They need to have a second vaccination two to four weeks later and need to be at least 16 weeks old to be sure their maternal immunity has worn off. They should then have a booster vaccination for all diseases six to twelve months later. After that, the boosters given will depend on the length of immunity.

179. PROTECTION

Vaccinating your pet not only protects your companion but also helps to protect sick or immunosuppressed animals and humans. Your vet will give vaccines only when needed, but in some cases, if you're worried, you can have your dog tested to see if any immunity to any particular disease has run out yet.

180. CHECK-UP

Don't forget that every time you go to get your dog a vaccination, your dog will have an examination from your vet. This is excellent for picking up subtle changes and early signs of disease that might go unnoticed. It's also an ideal time to talk about concerns and to check your dog's weight. It's not just about the booster!

181. WORMS

There are lots of different worms that can infect dogs and other animals. Some just cause a nuisance by eating your dog's food inside the intestine, but many cause serious damage in different organs, and some even kill animals.

182. LOCATION

The types of worms your dog may get depend on where you live, so it's important you know what is a problem in your area of the country. The most common worms are roundworms, tapeworms, hookworms, and whipworms.

183. ROUNDWORMS

The biggest problem for puppies and pregnant or nursing mothers is roundworms. These worms can cause intestinal problems and even blockages for the puppies. There can be poor weight gain.

184. HUMANS

Roundworms can also infect humans through contact with dog feces. Children are most at risk. The worm larvae migrate through the body and can damage organs and, though very rarely, cause blindness in children. This is why it's so important to pick up your dog's poop!

185. PREGNANCY

During pregnancy, worms from the bitch infect the puppies through the uterus and also, after birth, through the mother's milk. The mother should be treated for worms before mating and every day from 40 days of pregnancy until two days after birth. Only certain drugs are safe in pregnancy, so make sure you check with your vet first.

186. PUPPIES

Even with worm treatment, some worms may get to the puppies, so they need to be treated, too. Normally, the puppies should be treated every two weeks from 2 weeks old to 12 weeks old. Then, they should be treated monthly until 6 months of age, after which treatment is the same as that for an adult dog.

187. OTHER PARASITES

Worms are the most important parasite to guard puppies from, but young dogs can also get fleas, lice, and mites, depending on where they are being raised. Don't be afraid to have a good look through their fur and in their ears before you take them home.

188. MITES

Ear mites are not uncommon in puppies. If you notice your puppy shaking its head a lot, or scratching its ears, or if you see lots of wax, the problem could be mites. They are very uncomfortable for any dog, so see your vet for something safe to guard against mites, based on the age of the dog.

189. TICKS

Once your puppy starts going out, he or she could pick up ticks. These tend to be more common in woods, grassland, and areas where there is wildlife or livestock grazing.

190. UNLOVED!

Sadly for vets who love animals dearly, the feeling is not always mutual! Lots of animals can easily end up with negative associations about going to the vet. Being examined by a vet is also quite an odd experience for dogs. Getting puppies used to being handled can really help.

191. HANDLING

From when your puppy is as young as possible, try to do these things gently and calmly once a day: Lift your puppy's lips up and look at the teeth, open the mouth a little way and look inside, touch the ears and peek inside, run your hands all over the pup's body and legs, pick paws up and gently spread the toes, lift the tail, and look at the bottom. Then, give your pup a little fuss and a dog treat.

192. RELAXED

This routine will help your dog feel relaxed
when a vet or a nurse has to do these things,
and it will help you, too. If you think
something is wrong and need to
examine your dog, or even if
you just need to dry muddy
paws, it will make life
easier for you and more
relaxing for your dog.

193. FREQUENT FLYERS

If at all possible, take your dog
to the vet frequently, even
when the dog doesn't need to go. Get the dog weighed or just pop in
for a chat. Usually, your dog can have a treat from the office, and
the animal will also learn that the vet is not a scary place to be.

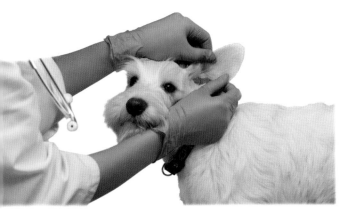

194. ESSENTIAL

Good nutrition is essential for puppies. Puppies have specific needs that are different from those of adult dogs. Young dogs need to grow at the right rate. Large-breed puppies that will be over 55 pounds (25 kilograms) when they are adults need large-breed puppy food.

195. GROWTH

Puppy food should be fed from weaning until around a year of age. This is a general guideline, but sometimes your vet may change the diet if your puppy is too fat or if something else is wrong. Never change to a non-puppy food without advice. Foods that are not balanced for growth can be disastrous in some cases.

196. JOINTS

Good puppy food can reduce joint and bone problems, help the immune system, and, believe it or not, make your puppy easier to train.

197. CALORIES

Growing up is hard work, and young animals as well as young humans need more calories than adults. Puppies need to eat more frequently than adults and need food that is digestible and calorific.

198. PROTEIN

Puppies need the most protein around the time of weaning, and the need reduces as they grow. Mom's milk is about 33 percent protein. Puppy foods should have 22 to 32 percent protein. Make sure you look at the levels on what's called a dry matter basis. This helps to compare wet and dry food equally.

199. FAT

This provides calories, helps carry some vitamins, and also provides fatty acids. Too much fat can make puppies obese, and this can cause growth problems in some dogs. The ideal level is 10 to 25 percent.

200. FATTY ACIDS

These are very important for lots of body functions, but for puppies the fatty acids are even more important. One fatty acid called DHA is needed for brain, eye, and hearing development. This is the fatty acid that can make your dog easier to train.

201. MINERALS

Puppies need more calcium and phosphorus than adults to help their skeletons grow and for lots of other cells too. BUT too much can be bad, and in large-breed puppies growth defects can be caused by too much calcium.

202. CALCIUM

Some people used to give large breeds extra calcium because they thought the dogs needed more for their big skeletons, but now we know this is totally wrong. Calcium and phosphorus content is most critical for growing pups. This is one reason that balanced, complete puppy foods are so important.

203. EXPERTS

Your vet is the best person to ask about which diets are best for your puppy.

204. PERCEPTION

Obesity is now a huge problem in dogs all over the world. Studies have shown that many people are now so used to seeing fat animals that they feel the larger sizes are normal. Slim dogs are sometimes mistaken for emaciated, when in fact they are the healthy ones!

205. BODY CONDITION SCORE

Body Condition Score (BCS) is a way that vets, nurses, and other professionals judge how fat or thin an animal is. Some use a scale of 1 to 5, and others, 1 to 9. Basically, the middle of the range of each (3 or 5) is just right. The lower the number, the thinner the animal is; and the higher the number, the more obese.

206. HEALTHIER

Knowing about BCS is excellent for owners, and being aware of your puppy's body condition as he or she grows is really important. Slim animals are much healthier than overweight ones.

207. BE AWARE

When you first have your puppy examined, ask your vet or nurse to show you how to do a BCS. All animals are individuals and will have slightly different calorie needs. You need to monitor your dog's weight to stay ahead of the game.

208. GUIDELINES

Most dog foods have a feeding guide on the bag or cans. This is usually a range of daily amounts for a certain weight of animal. Start in the middle of the range, and adjust the ration for your individual dog.

209. IDEAL WEIGHT

Always feed for the weight your animal SHOULD be. Ask your vet if you're not sure.

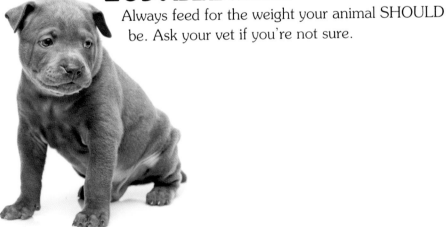

210. HUNGER

Remember that some dogs would eat all day every day given the chance, so don't get sucked in by those pleading eyes. Get into good habits right from the start. Preventing weight gain is so much easier than getting the extra weight off again.

211. HABITS

Don't feed your dog from the table or every time you eat, as the dog will expect to be fed, and mealtimes soon will become a slobbery nightmare for all concerned! If you want to feed your dog three or four times a day all its life, that's fine. It can help keep your dog satisfied. Make sure you split the ration, though. Don't feed extra.

212. FEELING FULLER

If your dog always seems ravenous, try soaking the dog's biscuits or try feeding canned food. The extra water helps fill a dog up and keeps hunger at bay.

213. GUILT

Lots of people lead busy lives these days, and finding time to exercise, play with, and interact with your dog can be difficult. Don't alleviate your guilt by giving snacks and treats. You'll simply create a vicious circle of obesity and lack of exercise. Make yourself go out with your dog, and you, your family, and the dog will all benefit!

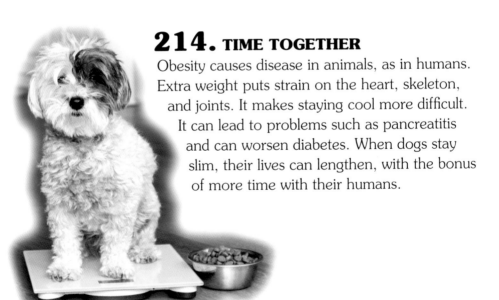

214. TIME TOGETHER

Obesity causes disease in animals, as in humans. Extra weight puts strain on the heart, skeleton, and joints. It makes staying cool more difficult. It can lead to problems such as pancreatitis and can worsen diabetes. When dogs stay slim, their lives can lengthen, with the bonus of more time with their humans.

215. EXPERTS

Feeding raw foods to dogs has become very popular in recent times, and some dogs do very well on such a diet, but there are several reasons that this is not ideal and why nutrition experts don't recommend it. The main reasons are as follows:

216. AVOID RAW FOOD REASON #1: PUBLIC HEALTH RISKS

Some meat used for human food have certain levels of salmonella and campylobacter in them. This is tolerated because it is accepted that humans cook their food. Dogs fed raw meat can shed these bacteria into the environment. This is dangerous, especially for children, older people, and people who are immune-suppressed, such as cancer patients.

217. AVOID RAW FOOD REASON #2: NOT WOLVES

Dogs are not like wolves, and raw foods are not a natural source of food for dogs, much like uncooked meats are not a natural choice for modern humans, compared to when early people lived in caves. Lots of dogs fed raw meats endure vomiting and diarrhea.

218. AVOID RAW FOOD REASON #3: BONES

Feeding bones to dogs can break teeth, lacerate mouths, cause very hard and painful stools, and even perforate intestines. This can be fatal if not treated quickly. It's best not to feed bones to dogs.

219. AVOID RAW FOOD REASON #4: UNBALANCED DIETS

Diets with high levels of meat are very unbalanced. Some raw foods have human vitamin and mineral tablets added to them, and the levels found in these foods can be very different from those needed by dogs, especially growing puppies. This can cause growth problems and vitamin deficiencies.

220. AVOID RAW FOOD REASON #5: ENERGY

Wolves cope with high-meat diets because they have much higher energy needs than dogs, and they eat much bigger volumes of food to keep their vitamin and mineral levels normal. If we fed dogs like this, they would all be morbidly obese!

221. AVOID RAW FOOD REASON #6: EVOLUTION

Some people think dogs shouldn't have carbohydrates because dogs are related to wolves.

In fact, dogs evolved beside humans and have eaten our scraps for thousands of years. Dogs have genes for digesting carbohydrates that wolves don't have.

222. AVOID RAW FOOD REASON #7: COOKING

If you really don't want to feed dog food to your dog, at least cook the meat to reduce the risks. Think very carefully about home cooking for a puppy, and seek specialist advice because your dog's nutrition is so important.

223. ARE YOU A MILLIONAIRE?

If not, then it's very wise to get some good pet insurance. Specialist vets are akin to human medical specialists. They have state-of-the-art equipment, such as MRI scanners and digital X-rays, and all manner of tests and surgeries are available for your pet. These are not cheap.

224. CHOICES

It's very sad to see clients faced with tough choices because of finances. By having some pet insurance, you can get help with the bigger bills and have peace of mind.

225. POLICIES

Knowing which company and policy to pick is a minefield. If money is tight, a basic package is better than nothing. Ideally, get a policy that covers each condition for life, not just your pet. This difference in wording can be very deceptive!

226. START EARLY

Take out the policy as early as you can because as soon as your dog gets ill, the related conditions may be excluded. Lots of vets and breeders offer a month of free insurance for puppies, so ask if that's an option, and make sure you're happy with the policy being offered.

227. CANCELLATION

Don't cancel a policy without thinking long and hard. Every vet will know someone who's canceled a policy because it was never used—and immediately something went wrong. The same applies to switching companies. If you've made a claim, the next company will exclude that condition, and you could regret it.

228. FRAUD

Please don't ask your vet to lie for an insurance company or change dates or records. Vets can be accused of insurance fraud.

229. ADVICE

If in doubt, talk to someone at your vet's practice. Vets and nurses deal with insurance companies day in, day out and have a good idea about which ones are good and bad, and which ones try to duck every claim. You wouldn't have a car or house without insurance, so why risk it with a beloved pet?

230. PROS AND CONS

As with many things in life, there are pros and cons and lots of different opinions when it comes to neutering. Talk to your vet about your breed of dog and which sex it is for all the details and to discuss the best time to do the operation.

231. NEUTERING

Neutering is the removal of the reproductive organs. For male dogs this means both testicles, and for females it means the ovaries and the uterus, or womb. Neutering stops dogs from being able to have or make babies, and it sometimes stops behaviors related to hormones.

232. WHICH WORD?!

Spaying is the word used for neutering a female dog and castration is the word used for males. The term neutering can be used for either to make life more simple!

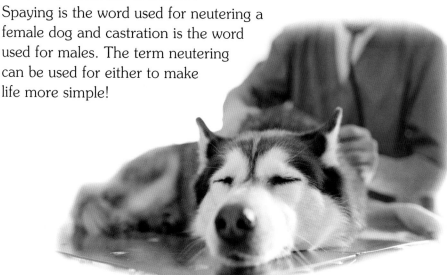

233. STAYING HOME

Neutering makes both sexes less likely to wander off in search of a mate and lessens the chance of the dog getting lost or injured.

234. MAMMARY CANCER

Spaying helps prevent aggressive mammary cancer in females. When it's done before the first season, spaying reduces the chance of mammary cancer to nearly zero.

235. PYOMETRA

Spaying stops a condition called pyometra. This is where the uterus gets infected and fills with pus. It makes females very ill and can be fatal. When this condition does occur, the uterus almost always has to be removed.

236. FAKING IT

Spaying greatly reduces the chance of false pregnancy. This is where the hormones of the bitch make her think and feel she is pregnant. She tends to make nests and may fill them with soft toys. She may start producing milk. False pregnancies are not dangerous but can be difficult to manage.

237. INCONTINENCE

On the other side of the coin, spayed bitches are more likely to become incontinent when older. Some breeds are more prone to this, so some vets recommend waiting until after their first season to spay them.

238. FALLACY

Some people say it's best for a bitch to have one litter. This is an old wives' tale and is untrue. Remember that pregnancy and birth are not without risks, and you also have to be able to find homes for the puppies.

239. TESTICULAR CANCER

Castration stops male dogs from getting testicular cancer, which can be fatal. Sometimes one or both testicles will not descend. This means the organs stay in the abdomen and don't appear in the scrotum. These testicles are much more likely to  become cancerous, so you should always have them removed.

240. PERIANAL CANCER

Castration reduces the risk of perianal tumors. These are cancers in the tissues and glands around the anus and tail, which can be very invasive and aggressive.

241. PROSTATITIS

Castration also greatly reduces the chances of prostate enlargement and inflammation. An enlarged prostate can cause pain and discomfort and can also make it difficult for your dog to do his business.

242. BLADDER STONES

Castration sometimes
protects against some
types of bladder crystals
and stones called struvite
and cystine.

243. HERNIAS

Dogs that are not castrated are more
likely to get weakening of the muscles around their bottoms as they
age. This can cause a perineal hernia, which is a bulging mass next
to the anus. This type of protrusion sometimes needs very complex
surgery for repair, but castration reduces the risk.

244. PROSTATE CANCER

On the con side, castrated male dogs are slightly more likely to get prostate cancer than entire or unneutered dogs. This is a rare disease, but it is more common in castrated dogs.

245. OTHER CANCERS AND JOINT DISEASE

Some studies now suggest that very early neutering in some breeds, especially larger ones, could make them more prone to cancers and also joint problems as they grow. Breed plays a big part in your decision and timing, so talk to your vet.

246.
RESPONSIBILITY

Millions of animals are put down each year because of unwanted litters. Besides the many benefits for your dog, neutering is the responsible thing to do.

247. TO NEUTER?

Neutering is often spoken about as a magic cure for behavioral issues, but this is rarely the case. Evidence points to some behavioral changes from neutering, but rarely are all cases improved. Dogs learn from their actions, so even if hormonally motivated, they have still learned the behaviors.

248. NEUTERING PROBLEMS

Occasionally, neutering a male or female dog can have a detrimental effect on behavior. A female that is undergoing phantom pregnancy, or a male dog that is displaying fear behaviors, can appear to have such behaviors worsened.

249. TOO LATE?

Before neutering for a behavior problem, the dog should always undergo specialist behavior assessment with a clinical animal behaviorist. Behavior modification is likely to help a dog and should be done before neutering, a permanent intervention, should be attempted.

250. MALES

Male dogs may compete as a result of hormonally motivated behaviors, such as fighting for access to females. They may lift their legs to urinate and may indulge in humping items. Neutering does not automatically stop these acts, as the dog has already learned to behave this way.

251. FEMALES

A female dog may suffer phantom pregnancy, where she nests and collects items into her bed. She may become defensive. This can be traumatic for her and for the family members who do not understand the cause. Neutering can prevent this, but usually the vet will wait until symptoms have completely vanished. This can take a long time.

252. FIGHTING

Female dogs within the same household may compete for space, items, people, and other resources, and this may sometimes be hormonally related. However, immediate neutering does not resolve the problem, and both dogs will need specialist behavioral help if they are to continue living together.

253. DIFFICULT DECISIONS

Without neutering, the effect of hormones on behavior can cause serious conflicts in multiple-dog households, sometimes ending with one dog being rehomed.

254. BENEFITS

In general, the health benefits of neutering, as well as removing the chance of unwanted puppies, outweighs the behavioral issues. However, each dog has to be assessed as an individual. The worst outcome would be neutering without assessment, potentially causing a behavior problem to increase.

ADOLESCENCE

255. SEXUAL MATURITY

Maturity varies among breeds and genders, but adolescence occurs around 4 to 12 months of age, with most dogs reaching sexual maturity around 10 to 12 months old.

256. GROWTH IN ADOLESCENCE

Dogs develop strength and skill, and their bodies change as they mature. Adult coats replace fluffy puppy coats. In some cases, this leaves a visible strip of longer adult fur that spreads across their backs. The dogs' limbs and muzzles grow, giving them a slightly gangly look for a while!

257. MARKING TERRITORY: MALES

Maturing dogs begin to scent mark for territory or to advertise themselves to mates. In males, lifting the rear leg and directing urine at a vertical surface characterizes this behavior.

258. MARKING TERRITORY: FEMALES

A female dog will find an area of scent from another dog and will squat to mark it with urine. These are normal behaviors for the maturing dog.

259. FIGHTING AND TERRITORIALITY

Both males and females can become sensitive to breeding competition, and this can lead to squabbles. Occasionally, this can lead to the dogs needing to be separated, but this situation can be improved with neutering. A clinical behaviorist is needed to help guide such important decisions.

ADULTHOOD

260. SCIENCE

The facts we know about food are amazing these days. By adjusting ingredients, food can achieve all sorts of goals and improvements. Food can keep normal dogs in top form and it can even help treat some diseases.

261. SLIM

Keep an eye on your dog's BCS, as mentioned in the puppy section. Adults need fewer calories than puppies do, so your dog can easily gain weight before the change is noticed. Prevention is much easier than cure.

262. ENERGY

Different breeds and lifestyles require very different energy levels. Some very energetic or working dogs find it difficult to keep weight on. Foods that are low fiber and high energy can really help.

263. FIBER

Higher-fiber foods are great for filling up hungry dogs and helping with weight loss. In some cases, these foods can also help anal gland problems, colitis, and constipation.

264. FAT

Some breeds of dog, such as cocker spaniels and schnauzers, are prone to pancreatitis, a very serious and painful disease. It's triggered by fatty foods. Foods that are low in fat keep the illness at bay.

265. BLADDER STONES

Dalmatians, bulldogs, schnauzers, and many more dogs can get bladder crystals and stones. Special diets have altered protein and mineral levels and change the pH of the urine in the bladder which helps to prevent bladder stones.

266. KIDNEYS

Kidney failure is often incurable, but diet can make a big difference to the length and quality of life for your companion. Kidney diets have lower protein and controlled phosphate levels, and are proven to prolong life.

267. LIVER

The liver is a powerful organ that performs many jobs. When it's damaged or failing, dropping protein levels and adding certain vitamins, minerals, and digestible fiber makes dogs feel better and live longer.

268. HEARTS

Heart disease is very common in some breeds, and fluid retention can put a lot of strain on a weak heart. Diets that have low salt levels and ingredients to help heart muscle stay healthy can help a lot.

269. ALLERGIES

Food allergies are pretty rare in dogs but can be serious when they occur. Skin and gut problems are common signs and can be life-threatening. Diets that avoid or alter certain ingredients can save these patients.

270. SKIN

Skin disease is fairly common in dogs and is caused by many things, such as pollen and mite allergies. Foods high in fatty acids calm inflamed skin and help strengthen the skin's defenses. Some ingredients can reduce histamine release and itchiness.

271. JOINTS

Lots of dogs suffer from arthritis, either due to their breed or just old age. Diets with high levels of fatty acids can soothe joints and slow down the damage of arthritis.

272. TEETH

Brushing your dog's teeth from a young age is by far the best way to keep the teeth clean and healthy. Some foods can help as well. Providing big kibbles that have to be chewed and less protein and minerals in your dog's diet can reduce tartar and plaque.

273. TAKE CARE

Foods can be powerful. Some prescription foods for diseases have been changed in ways that can be dangerous for certain dogs, especially if they have other diseases. Never feed a prescription food without your vet's approval.

274. HOT DOGS

Every year without fail, dozens of dogs die around the world from being left in cars. Even on cool, sunny days, the temperature inside a car can become deadly in a very short time. Even if you leave the windows cracked, you could kill your dog. Do NOT do it, EVER!

275. HEAT EXHAUSTION

Even dogs traveling in the back of the car can get heat exhaustion or heat stroke. This can be rapidly fatal. Just because you are chilling in the front with the air conditioning on doesn't mean your dog isn't gasping in the back.

276. WHAT TO DO

If you suspect your dog has heat exhaustion or stroke (gasping, mouth open, extreme panting, shaking), cooling is essential. Cold wet towels, a hosing off—anything you can do—you must drop your dog's body temperature. Go to a vet as quickly as possible.

277.
STICK
THROWING
You may not know it,
but many dogs are seriously
injured or killed by sticks every year.
As the dog catches up to the stick, the
bounce is awkward, and the dog runs onto
the stick and gets impaled.

278. STICK INJURIES
The stick can penetrate the mouth, neck, tongue, palate, and even the
brain. Please don't throw sticks for your dog!

279. VACCINATIONS
To avoid issues with any injuries from sticks or other objects, it's very
important to keep your dog's vaccines up to date. Some vaccinations
will need to be handled yearly. Others should be done every few years.
If you're worried about vaccinations, have your dog blood-tested to see
which ones are needed.

280. ROUNDWORMS

Most adult dogs will get roundworms from contact with dog poop or from eating wildlife, such as mice, from the environment. The infected dogs can also infect humans.

281. SIGNS

If dogs get worms, the signs vary. They could get pot-bellied, vomit, have diarrhea, become thin, or cough as the larvae migrate.

282. TAPEWORMS

Commonly spread by fleas, most tapeworms are not dangerous. However, worms in the genus Echinococcus are very dangerous and can infect and even kill humans. Controlling all worms is essential, especially if you take your dog abroad.

283. HEARTWORMS

These are spread only by infected mosquitoes and occur in certain
areas around the world. The adults live in the heart and surrounding
areas. They can be difficult to get rid of and can cause a lot of damage.

284. SIGNS OF HEARTWORMS

It can take months from the first bite to see the signs of Heartworms.
Coughing and not being able to exercise properly are common signs.

285. LUNGWORMS

This is an increasingly common problem in many areas. Dogs catch them by eating slugs or snails, sometimes accidentally while playing. The worms migrate through lots of areas of the body and can easily cause enough damage to kill a dog.

286. SIGNS OF LUNGWORMS

Because Lungworms go all through the body to get to the lungs, the signs vary. Look for wheezing, breathing problems, blood-clotting problems, blood in the urine, tiredness, nosebleeds, and problems exercising.

287. TREATMENT

Most worm infestations can be successfully treated if caught early. The drugs needed and the course of treatment will vary for the different types, but your vet will tell you what to do. Prevention is always better.

288. PREVENTION

There are plenty of drugs available these days for preventing worms. Some need to be given every few months, and some are given monthly. Not all treatments kill all worms, so you must talk to your vet about the recommendations for where you live.

289. TICKS

Ticks climb onto your dog
during outdoor activities.
They bury their heads
firmly in the dog's
skin to drink blood.
These creatures
vary greatly in size
and can be easy to
miss until they are engorged.
Ticks can cause fever and infection and also
spread serious diseases.

290. FLEAS

Fleas spend most of their lives off the dog, and for every flea you see
there are about 100 others in the house! They can cause irritation
in most dogs and severe allergies in some. All dogs get fleas. Just
because you don't see them doesn't mean they are not there. These
parasites also spread tapeworms.

291. CLUES

Flea dirt is a great clue to look for. Comb your dog's fur over a white
piece of kitchen paper. If you see black specks, moisten the paper.
Normal dirt will not change, but flea dirt, which is made of dried
blood, will make a red patch on the paper.

292. SCABS

Fleas cause itching in most dogs, especially around the head, neck, and tail. If you see bald patches and scabs in these areas, your dog is probably allergic or heavily infested.

293. LICE AND MITES

Less common than fleas and ticks, lice and mites can still be a problem. Mange from mites can be difficult to treat and can cause intense irritation and skin damage from itching and infection.

294. CONTROL

There are many sprays and spot treatments now that are very effective for the prevention and cure of these pesky critters. Always check with your vet. Ask what is safe to use, what the vet recommends, and how often to use it.

295. ANYTHING GOES!

There are many dogs that will eat anything and everything. The list of things vets have pulled from dog intestines is absolutely staggering, so never underestimate what dogs will do! They steal food and are inclined to eat other objects, too. Accidental poisoning is pretty common, but if you know what causes problems, you can keep the dogs in your life safe.

296. TREATS

People love to give their dogs treats and human snacks, and, as we said, some dogs will happily steal anything they can get their paws on. Sadly, several human foods are very poisonous to dogs, so be aware. Do your best to train your dogs not to eat things that they were not given to eat.

297. CHOCOLATE

Chocolate is very toxic to dogs. It contains theobromine, a relative of caffeine, and dogs are very sensitive to it. The darker the chocolate, the more theobromine it contains. Easter and Christmas always see a rise in related cases. It causes vomiting, diarrhea, and seizures, and it can be fatal. Caffeine is also toxic.

298. GRAPES AND RAISINS

Lots of people like to give fruit as treats, but grapes are deadly to dogs. They cause kidney failure. Some dogs seem to be much more sensitive than others. First signs are vomiting, followed by lethargy, excessive thirst, and urination. Then, the kidneys shut down, and there is coma and death. Best avoided! Don't forget foods that contain raisins, too.

299. ONIONS AND GARLIC

These foods cause gut irritation but can also affect the blood and cause anemia. Onions are the most toxic. The poisoning is usually slow, so signs don't appear until a few days afterward.

300. XYLITOL

The sweetener Xylitol is found in many foods and sugar substitutes. In dogs, this sweetener makes the body release insulin. This drops blood sugar rapidly, so much so that dogs can quickly go into a coma and die. Ingesting it can also cause liver failure.

301. OTHER FOODS

Other foods that can be poisonous are raw bread dough, alcohol, macadamia nuts, blue cheese, and any foods that have gone moldy. Keep all these foods away from your dog.

302. PESTICIDES

Rats, mice, slugs, and snails are pests for a lot of humans, and it is common to set out poisons for them. Many pest poisons are toxic for dogs, too. Slug bait and rat poison can easily kill dogs. Avoid them if at all possible.

303. MEDICATION

Dogs are like kids. They'll learn to open cupboards, reach high, and nose about in handbags! Many dogs each year are poisoned by both human and animal medication. Keep them all well out of the way. This includes your own recreational or prescribed drugs.

304. HOUSEHOLD CHEMICALS

Any manner of household and garden chemical
can be swallowed, chewed, and licked by your
dog. Keep everything locked away, and don't
leave buckets of household chemicals around.

305. PLANTS AND ANIMALS

Some plants, such as daffodils and other
spring bulbs, can be dangerous. In many
countries around the world, there are also
venomous animals to watch out for. Keep
your dog well trained, so you can call the
dog away from danger if you need to.

306. WHAT TO DO?

If you think your dog has been
poisoned, go straight to your vet.
Take the packet or container if you
can. There are very few antidotes, but
supportive treatment can save lives, and
the earlier the better.

307. BE SAFE

If you're ever worried or unsure about something, it's better to be on the safe side—so go and see your vet. Lots of people have later regretted that they didn't.

308. BE OBSERVANT

The more you know what is normal for your dog, the sooner you will spot changes or odd signs. Try to have a rough idea of your dog's normal drinking and eating habits and amounts. How often does the dog relieve itself? What do the poops normally look like? Keep doing the checks mentioned in the puppy section. This way, you'll find lumps and bumps that fur might hide.

309. WHEN TO GO TO THE VET #1: APPETITE

Some dogs aren't very driven by food, while others would eat all day. If your dog's appetite goes down, or your dog goes off food altogether for more than a day, seek advice. A reduced appetite could be a sign of fever, pain, or any number of infections and conditions. An increased appetite can also be a sign of disease, such as Cushing's or diabetes.

310. WHEN TO GO TO THE VET #2: DRINKING

Normal water needs for dogs is about 0.5 to 1 ounce per pound (30 to 60 ml per kg) each day. The amount they drink will vary depending on their level of exercise and if they are given wet food, so try to have an idea of what is normal for your dog. More than 1.5 ounces per pound (90 ml per kg) each day is not normal. Increased thirst is a sign of many diseases, such as kidney disease, Cushing's, diabetes, pyometra, and high blood calcium. Always see your vet if you think your dog is drinking more than usual.

311. WHEN TO GO TO THE VET #3: VOMITING

Vomiting is serious because if an animal can't keep fluids down it becomes dehydrated very quickly. If your dog vomits frequently for more than 12 hours, see a vet immediately. Vomiting very soon after food, even if your dog is alert, can be a sign of a blockage in the intestines and needs investigating. If your dog seems very lethargic and vomits, go to the vet straight away.

312. WHEN TO GO TO THE VET #4: DIARRHEA

Diarrhea is very common in dogs. Watery, profuse diarrhea is more worrying than slimy, soft poops. If your dog has very dark or black diarrhea, your dog may be bleeding internally. If you see blood, go to your vet. If your dog is bright and still eating, you can wait a day or two to see if the diarrhea settles. If more than 48 hours passes, or if your dog seems unwell, go straight away.

313. WHEN TO GO TO THE VET #5: STRAINING TO URINATE

A dog can get urinary infections just like a human can, and you may notice your dog trying to pee but passing only a few drips. Some dogs also get bladder stones. A blocked bladder is a medical emergency. If you ever think your dog can't pass urine or is having difficulty, go straight to your vet.

314. WHEN TO GO TO THE VET #6: BLOAT

Some dogs get gastric dilation or bloat. If a dog gets very swollen, normally after eating, or if the dog is trying to be sick but nothing is coming up, seek immediate veterinary advice. Swollen stomachs can twist, and this is rapidly fatal. Only about 50 percent of dogs experiencing twists survive, so the earlier the dog is seen, the better.

315. WHEN TO GO TO THE VET #7: LUMPS

Lumps can be signs of cancer, but many lumps are nothing to worry about. In general, if the lumps are slow-growing, smooth, painless, not firmly attached to the tissue around them, and not ulcerated, they are benign. The opposite means possible problems. If you're ever unsure, get them checked.

316. WHEN TO GO TO THE VET #8: BALD PATCHES

Hair loss is normal, and many owners are constantly covered in dog hair! However, if you see bald patches, with or without scabs and itching, get your dog checked out. Hair loss can be a sign of parasites and allergies, but also some hormonal problems, too.

317. WHEN TO GO TO THE VET #9: SNEEZING

Sneezing is unusual in dogs and should usually be investigated. It may be a sign of something stuck in the nose, especially if the sneezing starts very suddenly on a walk. Chronic sneezing with any kind of mucus coming from one or both sides of the nose should definitely be investigated, as should any swellings on the muzzle.

318. WHEN TO GO TO THE VET #10: COUGHING

Normal breathing is fairly silent, so if you hear any coughing, wheezing, or snoring, you should see a vet. Breathing changes could be because of chest infections, but coughing can also be a sign of heart failure, so don't ignore it.

319. WHEN TO GO TO THE VET #11: SMELLS!

Lots of things can change the way your dog smells. Watch out for smelly ears, skin, and breath. These can be signs of ear mites, infections, skin allergies, dental disease, and so on.

320. WHEN TO GO TO THE VET #12: LETHARGY

If your dog seems very tired or reluctant to go for a walk, you should have your dog checked over. It may be a sign of heart problems but can also be from anemia or even bleeding internally in the case of some tumors.

321. WHEN TO GO TO THE VET
#13: WEIGHT

Weigh your dog regularly at the vet. Weight loss is a common sign of disease and can go unnoticed to begin with, especially with very hairy breeds. Weight gain may be just a matter of feeding too much, and you can correct it, but it may also be a sign of thyroid problems or other hormonal diseases that need a vet's treatment.

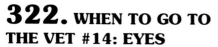

322. WHEN TO GO TO
THE VET #14: EYES

Eyes can easily get permanently damaged if left untreated. Look out for the whites of the eye being red or bloodshot, discharge from one or both eyes, swollen lids, or squinting. Squinting or half-closed eyes are usually signs of pain.

323. WHEN TO GO TO THE VET #15: TWITCHES AND FITS

Any neurological signs should be treated as an emergency. Seizures can be life-threatening. A tilted head, weakness, knuckle dragging, facial drooping, or twitching can be signs of brain or spinal cord problems. Don't leave them unexamined for too long.

324. DON'T HESITATE

Of course, there will be many other things that may prompt you to go to the vet. If you are ever in doubt, don't hesitate.

SUPER SENIORS

325. TEETH

Older dogs are very likely to have some teeth problems, including tartar, plaque, or gum disease. Brushing throughout life helps, but sometimes they'll need extractions or tartar removal. Many dogs with infected gums suffer in silence and really benefit from a dental clean and antibiotics.

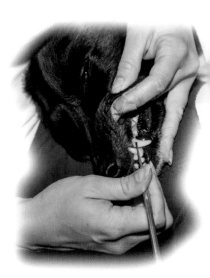

326. JOINTS

Arthritis is very common in older dogs. Hips, elbows, and knees are most affected. Certain diets, joint supplements, and painkillers can make life much more comfortable for senior dogs.

327. LUMPS

Fatty lumps called lipomas are very common in older dogs. Look back at what was said before about the rules for lumps. Lipomas are usually smooth and slow-growing, and they glide about a little when touched.

328. WHEN TO ACT ON LUMPS

Lipomas rarely cause problems unless they get very big or are in an awkward place, such as the armpit. If you're ever in any doubt about a lump and feel it could be cancerous, go to your vet.

329. CANCER

As well as lump-type growths, older dogs are more likely to get cancer internally. Watch out for weight loss, tiredness, coughing, and swollen bellies. Many cancers can be treated, and the earlier they are found the better.

330. KIDNEY FAILURE

If your dog starts drinking and peeing a lot, loses weight, or goes off food, it could be a sign of kidney disease. Diet and medication can help prolong life.

331. LIVER FAILURE

Yellow eyes and gums, vomiting, loss of appetite, and a swollen abdomen can all be signs of liver problems. Your vet can use medicines to help with some liver diseases.

Feeding a lower-protein liver diet in lots of small meals also helps reduce the strain on the liver.

332. HEART FAILURE

Some breeds of dog are very prone to heart disease, but any older dog of any kind can be affected. Coughing and not being able to exercise are common signs of this issue. Medication can make a massive difference to life expectancy.

333. HORMONES

Diabetes and other hormonal or endocrine diseases, such as thyroid problems and Cushing's, are more common in older dogs. Look out for weight gain, increased thirst, and changes in appetite and fur.

334. BREATHING

Coughing, wheezing, and even gagging can be signs of breathing problems or issues such as collapsing windpipes. These can be very serious, so always seek veterinary advice.

335. NAILS

Many dogs virtually never need their nails cut because walking keeps them short. Older dogs that don't exercise as much can get very overgrown nails, so keep an eye on them. Ask your vet if you think your dog's nails are too long.

336. GROOMING

Older dogs are less supple and may find grooming themselves more of an issue. Hair is more likely to be matted and clumped and could be uncomfortable. Regular, gentle grooming will help.

337. EARLY DETECTION

With most mammals, including humans, diseases and organ failure sometimes don't show signs until it's too late to help. Your vet may recommend regular blood tests for mature pets every year or half-year. These are very important for finding diseases early, when you still have a chance to act.

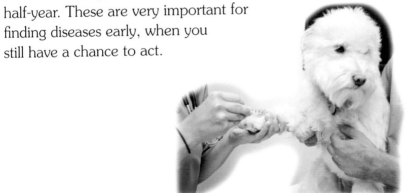

338. AGING GRACEFULLY

Changes come with old age, and dogs show many different behaviors related to their later years. They may take longer to pick up new skills, or they may forget locations and pre-existing training.

339. BEHAVIORAL CHANGES IN OLD AGE

As a dog's hearing, scent, vision, and touch senses deteriorate, this can affect how the dog perceives the world. Owners often notice physical changes, such as their companion's slower movement upon rising, but forget that emotions and behavior are also impacted.

340. MENTAL AGILITY

Older dogs are capable of learning new skills but may need additional practice. They may not problem-solve as quickly as they used to, so be patient. When teaching new behaviors, give additional guidance and more repetitions to help older dogs stay confident. The practice keeps their lives interesting. Avoid punishing them for slips in memory.

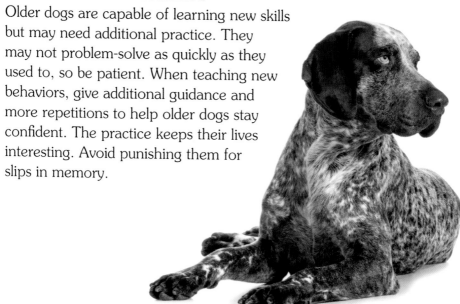

341. ACCIDENTS

Older dogs may need to relieve themselves more frequently or may not be able to quickly access the area where it usually goes, so provide extra opportunities to go outside. Accidents may occur. Older female dogs, especially those that are spayed, may leak a little urine at times. See your vet for help.

342. A YOUNGER COMPANION?

You may add another dog to the family, but your older dog needs careful preparation. Elderly dogs do not like being bounced around by a puppy! They may not appreciate having to share their space. Provide a quiet space for your elder to retreat to, undisturbed.

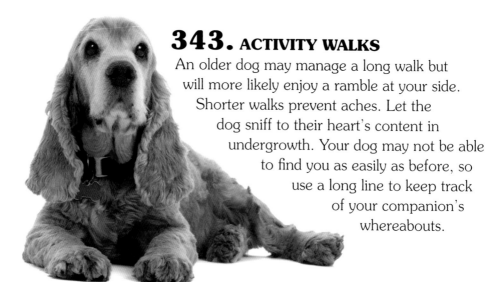

343. ACTIVITY WALKS

An older dog may manage a long walk but will more likely enjoy a ramble at your side. Shorter walks prevent aches. Let the dog sniff to their heart's content in undergrowth. Your dog may not be able to find you as easily as before, so use a long line to keep track of your companion's whereabouts.

344. CANINE COGNITIVE DYSFUNCTION

The brain deteriorates with age, and capacity can also diminish. Your dog may not be able to recognize familiar people any longer. An aging dog might not sleep at night, becoming distressed instead and barking when you are not in the room. The dog may worry when separated from you, or stare into space for long periods.

345. MANAGING SENILITY

Aim to keep to existing routines, and look out for distress signals, such as panting, yawning, or licking lips. Your old dog will sleep very deeply and may be hard to rouse from slumber, so go gently.

346. BRAIN FOOD

Some companies make foods rich in antioxidants and fatty acids, which have been proven to reverse some of the changes seen with brain aging and to help slow down the progression. Talk to your vet about whether these foods would suit your dog.

347. SEVERE BEHAVIORAL SYMPTOMS

Separation distress can appear as part of cognitive dysfunction and can be difficult to resolve. Your dog may defecate or urinate in front of you, not realizing the urge and forgetting to ask to go out. If you notice this or see repetitive behaviors, such as pacing or circling, ask your vet or clinical behaviorist for advice.

348. DEALING WITH LOSS

Should your elderly dog pass away, be aware that you and any other family members and pets will need time and space to grieve. Prepare for everyone to get the extra support needed to recover from the loss.

349. NEEDS

As dogs age, they need fewer and fewer calories on the whole, so remember to watch their weight. As they tend to get stiff with arthritis, it's even more important to see them slim.

350. FEEDING

Talk to your vet about switching to a higher-fiber diet if your dog is hungry on smaller rations. Splitting the ration into three or four meals a day also helps keep the dog feeling fuller.

351. MATURE OR SENIOR

Most good food companies make diets especially for older animals, often called mature or senior diets. These tend to have lower protein and mineral amounts, to be gentler on older organs.

352. UNDERWEIGHT

With age and some diseases, dogs become underweight. As said before, if you notice weight loss, go straight to your vet.

353. EXERCISE

Your older dog may not want or need to go out for walks as long or as often as before. If you find yourself dragging your dog out for a walk, ease off and try to listen to your companion to decide how much to do.

354. LITTLE AND OFTEN

In general, with older dogs it's better to go for more frequent, shorter walks than one or two long ones. This keeps them mobile without overdoing it.

355. SWIMMING

If you have a dog that likes swimming and you can do it safely, it's great exercise in moderation for older dogs. Just as for humans, non-weight-bearing exercise can help with joint problems.

356. PRESCRIPTION FOODS

At this stage, your vet may be more likely to recommend a specific food if your dog is unwell. Joints, kidneys, livers, and hearts may be showing signs of wear and tear, and certain diets can really benefit these conditions.

357. INEVITABLE

We have amazing medical and surgical expertise nowadays, just as in human medicine, but death is sadly inevitable. At least for our pets we can offer a dignified end.

358. HEARTBREAK

Every owner who has ever said goodbye to a beloved pet will have felt the heartbreak that this brings but also the feelings of guilt because it is often the owner's decision.

359. TALK

The death can dwell in your thoughts for months, so make sure you talk to your family and friends, and also your veterinary team.

360. ULTIMATE KINDNESS

You make your dog's life as great as you can, and allowing a pain-free death and an end to suffering is the ultimate kindness you can offer.

361. GOING PEACEFULLY

Many owners wish their dogs would pass away quietly in their sleep. Sadly, it is very rare for natural deaths to happen this way.

362. KNOW WHAT TO EXPECT

Try to find out what actually happens if and when your dog is put to sleep. Many owners dread or fear the process, but if you know what to expect you will cope much better with it.

363. HOME OR AWAY

All owners should have the right to manage euthanasia as they want or need to. If you'd like your dog to be at home in a familiar place with as many or as few people as you want, then don't be afraid to ask. There are specific vets who will be able to accommodate your wishes.

364. SHOULD I STAY OR SHOULD I GO?

Some owners are desperate to stay with their pets at the end, but many wish to remember them as they were or simply can't face the prospect of staying. This is YOUR choice, and no one will think any less of you, whatever you decide.

365. HELPFUL INFORMATION

There are a variety of online resources available to give you help and advice when the time comes. You can find out what will actually happen when your dog is put to sleep. If you're worried about staying, this may help you decide.

366. BURIAL

Depending on where you live, you may have the choice of burying your dog in the garden. Many owners like knowing a pet is there, perhaps in a spot the dog always chose to enjoy sunshine. It may sound obvious, but make sure you consider the logistics of the hole, especially if you have a large dog.

367. CREMATION

Almost every vet will offer a cremation service, individual or not. An individual cremation is as it sounds, and you will have the choice to have your dog's ashes back. If you choose a normal cremation, the crematorium will dispose of your dog's ashes.

368. MONEY MATTERS

Like all things in life, death also comes at a price. Talking about euthanasia costs, billing, the timing of payments, and the costs of cremation can be very difficult for both you and your veterinary team. Discuss costs and settlement early on to avoid discussing it when you are upset.

369. COPING

Everyone grieves in different ways, and your vet will have seen every reaction, so don't feel self-conscious about being upset.

370. GRIEF COUNSELING

In many countries, there are now specialist services to help pet owners through grief. Ask your vet or go online if you are struggling to come to terms with the loss.

371. REMEMBER THE GOOD TIMES

This may sound silly, but in the weeks and months afterward, look at photos of your dog when younger, talk about it all with friends and family, and think about the funny and cheeky things your dog did. Laughter and happiness are great antidotes to sadness.

A DOG'S SENSES

372. DID YOU SEE THAT?

Dogs use their eyesight very much like humans do, to focus on objects of interest and to convey information to the brain for interpretation. However, dogs' eyes are more suited to the purpose of hunting and tracking moving prey, or, sometimes, moving toys!

373. VISUAL ACUITY

This term refers to the ability to focus. Dogs cannot focus on items closely, unlike humans, as canine eyes are constructed differently. Dogs have a visual streak, an arrangement of cells in the eyes that allows exceptional peripheral vision and movement detection, essential for a predator that hunts.

374. FIELD OF VISION

With eyes positioned to the sides of the head in most breeds, dogs have a wide visual field and may notice movement behind them. This sensitivity can be surprising to humans, whose eyes are positioned to the front and who focus on objects ahead.

375. SPOT THE BALL

Dogs find it easy to spot a thrown ball in motion, but may not see a ball as easily when it is still and in front of them. As cursorial predators, dogs evolved limbs adapted for running and for chasing prey. Prey species such as rabbits adapted ways to keep still or to freeze so they can avoid being caught!

376. IS SHARP EYESIGHT A PROBLEM?

The optokinetic reflex, which is how eyes reflexively track movement, is more sensitive in a dog than in a human. This explains why a dog may suddenly snap at a fly or may become startled by sudden, unusual movement, such as a plastic bag blowing in the breeze.

377. CAN DOGS SEE TELEVISION?

Newer, high-quality digital images on television make it much easier for dogs to follow movement on the screen. Dogs are stimulated when recognizing shapes such as other dogs or sheep, and the high-pitched noises that accompany such images can cause dogs to react.

378. TASTE TEST

A dog has a much weaker taste sense compared to that of a human, with fewer than 200 taste buds compared to the human's 9,000.

379. TASTE OR SMELL?

It may be that the dog's sense of smell compensates for any comparative weakness once the item is in his or her mouth.

380. WHY DO DOGS EAT DISGUSTING THINGS?

A dog will happily dine on nonfood items. Coprophagia, where a dog eats the poop of other animals and even its own, baffles most humans! For the dog, the feces may just smell like food. If this occurs, check with your vet, as feces can transfer parasites.

381. UNSAFE EATING

Consuming toxic items can lead dogs into serious trouble. Human families often leave foods that are lethal to dogs in range, such as chocolate. Sometimes, dogs are given the wrong foods by mistake. As scavengers, dogs will eat most things. Just because dogs want to eat something doesn't mean it is good for them!

382. TOUCH SENSITIVE

Each dog likes different amounts of tactile contact. Some love to be stroked, and others find that uncomfortable. Never assume that a dog enjoys petting. Allow the dog to approach you, and never reach over the dog's head to stroke it. This may be seen as a threat.

383. SOUND SEEKING

A dog's sense of hearing helps it navigate toward its goals, detecting and interpreting sound as it is funneled in the ears.

384. EARS!

Dogs' ears take various shapes, from erect and upstanding to long and floppy, but their hearing is excellent no matter how their ears look.

385. HIGH-PITCH HEARING

Dogs detect many sounds that humans cannot, from the scratching and squeaks of tiny vermin to the noises of possible intruders. Some dogs are especially sensitive and will alert their owners with excitable barking.

386. HEARING RANGES

A dog can hear intervals of 67 to 45,000 Hz, compared to a human's 64 to 23,000 Hz, but this varies according to the breed and the size and shape of the dog's ears. Human hearing is relatively poor, and we forget that some sounds can be unpleasant to a dog's sensitive ears.

387. DEAF DOGS

A dog that cannot hear makes use of its other senses and still makes an excellent and trainable pet and family friend. Hereditary deafness is often related to white pigmentation and piebald coats, but it is also common to breeds such as the Doberman pinscher.

388. TRAINING WITH SOUNDS

A high-pitched dog whistle is often used to alert a dog for training, but a special whistle is not always needed, other than over long distances. A dog can be trained using human voices for cues.

389. A DOG'S SENSE OF SMELL

Dogs are renowned for their incredible sense of smell, which can detect and analyze many different scents as well as differentiating between them.

390. UNDERSTANDING OUR DOGS

Humans often fail to imagine how the sense of smell can both help and hinder dogs in our world, which is filled with a wide mixture of different types of scent.

391. NOSE CONSTRUCTION

Dogs' noses are delicately constructed, and they must never be forced to sniff or contact strong aromas.

392. SCENT ANALYSIS

A dog's nasal cavity contains a rich supply of nerves linking to the olfactory center in the brain. The vomeronasal organ, or Jacobson's organ, allows the analysis of scent, primarily of pheromones carrying information about emotions and mating.

393. PHEROMONES

These substances communicate sexual factors, such as a dog's maturity or whether a female is in heat nearby, as well as conveying information about marked territory or aggressive intent. Recently, pheromones have been artificially created in an effort to calm dogs that are stressed.

394. WHEN A DOG SNIFFS

When your dog sniffs heartily at the air, the nostrils dilate and the air is split for the dual purposes of an olfactory analysis of scents and respiratory needs, or breathing.

395. SCENT INFORMATION

Dogs investigate each other's rear ends when they meet. Dogs will also roll in strong-smelling items, such as the excrement of other animals or even rotten carcasses. This may be to disguise their scents or to mark the new scent as theirs.

396. TRACKING AND SEARCHING

Dogs' incredible ability to follow and analyze scent is used to locate lost items and people, and to track paths. Dogs may work to locate drugs, money, or banned food items at country border controls. The animals can easily perform these tasks, and their training helps them communicate such information to their human teachers.

397. SCENT MATCHING

Dogs can recognize one scent and compare it to others, locating the matching scent from a choice of many.

BEHAVIOR AND TRAINING

398. TRAINING

This is the means of directing your dog's behavior. Training lets you and your dog meet common goals. It is not simply tricks or afterthought.

399. POSITIVE REINFORCEMENT

Training based in positive reinforcement uses items or events to reinforce or reward behavior. If an outcome is rewarding for the dog, the dog will repeat the behavior. If the outcome is unrewarding, it is less likely that the behavior will be repeated.

400. REPETITION

Dogs are well aware of what benefits them. Often trainers use repetition to ensure that dogs have plenty of practice at desired behaviors. Repetition must be consistent, or the dogs become confused.

401. PUNISHMENT

Using unacceptable aversive methods, such as physical striking, shouting, electric shock, or pulling sharply on the dog's lead, can harm a dog physically, through spinal or eye damage due to the sudden impact of the movement, and emotionally, by creating fear and frustration.

402. THE TRAINING ENVIRONMENT IS IMPORTANT

A dog should be trained in a context where little else is happening to prevent distraction or confusion.

403. MARKERS

A marker indicates when a dog has made a correct choice.

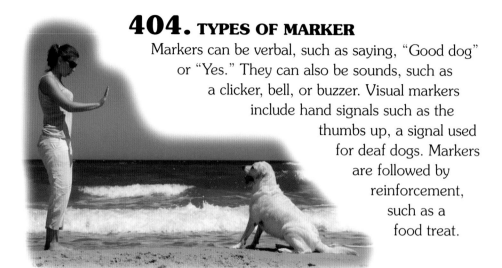

404. TYPES OF MARKER

Markers can be verbal, such as saying, "Good dog" or "Yes." They can also be sounds, such as a clicker, bell, or buzzer. Visual markers include hand signals such as the thumbs up, a signal used for deaf dogs. Markers are followed by reinforcement, such as a food treat.

405. STRUCTURE

Training follows this format: 1) gaining the dog's attention, 2) a cue or an instruction from the trainer, 3) the desired behavior, 4) the marker, 5) some reinforcement or reward. This simple structure allows all owners to teach new skills to their dogs without confusion.

406. TIMING

Accurate timing is essential so that the dog can link what the owner is trying to teach to the "wages" being offered. If the trainer is too slow, the dog cannot learn that a behavior is getting "paid" with food. The dog may not link the reward with the desired behavior.

407. PRACTICE IN NEW PLACES

Once the dog learns the trained behavior, the teaching is moved to a new setting and repeated. This assures that the trained behavior is thoroughly understood.

408. TRAINING IS ESSENTIAL FOR WELFARE

Professionals agree that training is fundamental for your dog's well-being. It allows for essential husbandry behavior, such as training the dog to let someone clip its nails.

409. USEFUL SKILLS

Training is beneficial because it provides useful behaviors, such as sitting instead of jumping up at visitors, or walking calmly on a lead in public. A dog will always be busy learning, and training is a dog's "employment." The dog doesn't become "self-employed," learning unwanted lessons.

410. WHY DO DOGS CHASE?

As well as scavenging for food and interesting items, dogs can also chase and hunt. In some dogs, especially working breeds, this instinct drives them to look for opportunities to behave as the predators they are. This can lead to serious problems.

411. PREDATORY SEQUENCE

This pattern of behaviors is familiar to the trained eye. To catch prey, dogs follow some or all of this sequence: Orient. Eye. Stalk. Chase. Grab/Bite. Kill. Dissect. Consume. Of course, most dogs no longer reach the final parts of the sequence. We have taught them to retrieve things instead.

412. BREED BEHAVIOR PATTERNS

Though not present in every dog, behavior patterns such as these are more prevalent in working dogs such as collies, which are skilled at herding and stalking other animals. Terriers will shake vermin wildly, which is an efficient killing method for rats.

413. CHASING ENJOYMENT

Racing after potential prey, whether it's birds, rabbits, mice, or even deer, can be exhilarating. Even if the dog does not catch the target, the chase itself is rewarding, leading the dog to seek further chasing opportunities. This can put the dog at risk.

414. PREVENTING CHASING

After learning the powerful rewards inherent in chasing, a dog will often seek it out at every juncture. Never allow your dog to freely chase, especially not when young. Instead, work on establishing a strong recall, so the dog comes back to you, no matter what temptations lie ahead.

415. CONTROLLED CHASING

It is unrealistic to think that a dog with a strong urge to chase can never be allowed to run after things. Instead, you must focus the dog on chasing games with a toy that you control. Your dog can fulfill the chase impulse and remain satisfied, without the risks of chasing live prey.

416. RETRIEVAL WORK

Teaching a dog to fetch means that even though allowed to chase away from you, your dog is ready to return. After catching or fetching the object that is tossed, your dog does not continue to run away. This is an enjoyable activity for both dog and owner in partnership.

417. CHASING AND GRABBING IN PLAY

Dogs love to chase one another, but this can lead to rough and

uncontrolled pursuit. For the dog being chased, this can be highly threatening. It may lead to a damaging grab or bite as the chasing dog attempts to catch the victim.

418. CONTROLLING CHASE-PLAY

Dogs should be trained not to chase one another for long periods without coming back when called. Short play sessions prevent bad chase habits from developing. Dogs playing healthy chase games should take turns being the chaser and the chasee.

419. RESOURCE GUARDING

A dog has a natural instinct to hold onto items considered valuable. This wish is related to survival needs. Problems occur when the dog is confronted and thus feels forced to defend a location or to prevent possessions from being taken away.

420. VALUABLE ITEMS

As scent-driven creatures, dogs can assign value to items we humans may otherwise disregard. Used tissues, worn socks, food aromas in the air, even garden snails, can all smell tempting to a canine. In turn, the dog may decide to protect such "valuable" objects.

421. DEFENDING RESOURCES

If a dog feels threatened, it may leave the area. However, this is less likely if the dog doesn't want to be moved from a comfortable location or fears that an item will be taken away. Then, the dog will likely defend the resources.

422. AGGRESSIVE BEHAVIOR

Dogs may choose to leave an area or let people take away their valued prizes. However, many dogs will growl and attempt to snap or bite in an effort to prevent this potential loss. This is usually successful!

423. ESCALATION OF GUARDING BEHAVIORS

If a dog is repeatedly punished, has valued items taken away, or is forced to move from favored places, the animal learns to resist. Your dog may hide with items or chase people away from certain locations. The guarding behaviors escalate until the dog is successful.

424. HANDS MUST GIVE

Human hands should not be used to smack or to snatch or to show who is the boss. Instead, our hands should be used for giving. This teaches the dog to not fear hands or guard items. Our hands can offer a tasty treat in a swap or to entice a dog to move.

425. HIGH-RISK BEHAVIORS

Dogs are good at working out what people are about to do and may learn to guard and defend large areas and a wide range of items. They may feel protective over the barest scent of an item. You must consult a clinical behaviorist for help with related issues.

426. PREVENTING RESOURCE GUARDING

All dogs have the potential to develop defensive behaviors of this type, even from early puppyhood. It can be hard to prevent it, but the problem can be effectively managed.

427. SWAP, DON'T SNATCH!

Always swap items, never spank or shout, and call your dog to you rather than pushing and shoving. All these rules can prevent problems from developing.

428. PROTECTING VISITORS, THE ELDERLY, AND CHILDREN

Should your dog protect your home, you must establish safety measures for anyone approaching. Delivery people are especially at risk. Lock all gates, place postboxes on external walls, and do not allow your dog access to areas where people approach.

429. FEARS

The feeling of fear is a normal reaction designed to keep every dog safe from harm. Alarming or scary events create either an impulse to flee or to stay and put up a defense. A dog may freeze in fear, or may suddenly scratch or sniff frantically. These are known as displacement behaviors, or fidgeting!

430. ANXIETY

A feeling of anxiety occurs when a dog predicts or recalls a previously fearful event, even if it is not recurrent. This creates problems when a dog generalizes past fear to a wide number of similar situations. The dog may show all the physical signs of fear and attempt to put up a defense or escape.

431. PHOBIA

Strong dread develops when a dog's quality of life is severely affected by fears and anxieties. Usually a phobia has to do with a specific stimulus, such as the noise of fireworks, but it can become impossible for the dog to function normally as a result of this kind of reaction.

432. TYPES OF FEAR OR PHOBIA

Dogs may fear situations that have previously created pain or alarm. This includes sudden events that startled them, attacks by other dogs, loud noises that hurt their ears, or being left alone and panicking as a result of the sudden loss.

433. FEAR DUE TO LACK OF EARLY SOCIALIZATION

Commonly, dogs originating from puppy farms or breeders or owners that did not socialize them develop fears and phobias. This is caused by the dogs' lack of experience at the crucial early socialization stage and is extremely difficult to resolve. These dogs need constant desensitization.

434. SEPARATION DISTRESS

As social creatures, dogs usually enjoy company and form attachments with people and other dogs. Sadly, dogs are frequently left alone, due to modern lifestyles. The dogs feel abandoned and may bark, howl, or damage doors and dig carpets in efforts to reunite with their owners.

435. NOISE PHOBIA

Dogs have sensitive hearing and may find loud or sudden sounds painful and aversive. Such responses are natural, but a phobia can develop to include similar noises. For example, gunshots or fireworks can scare a dog, and a balloon popping or door slamming has the same percussive nature.

436. DIG, DIG, DIG!

Dogs naturally dig and explore interesting scents. This is a natural behavior, so don't be hard on them when they start.

437. CAUTION AROUND DIGGING

Be careful that your dog is not digging up bulbs to eat, as these are toxic!

438. PROVIDE A DIGGING PIT

You can easily provide a sandpit or an area of the garden where you can clean up any mess easily enough with a broom. Bury toys in this area to encourage your dog to dig there.

439. PROTECT THE GARDEN

You may have a lovely garden, but your dog doesn't realize how much you love it. Fence in or wire off areas where your dog may cause damage.

440. SCAVENGING

Dogs eat things while on walks and take things from trash cans and other places where garbage collects. This is part of their natural instincts but can be dangerous.

441. PREVENTION

Teach your dog to come back and sit at every opportunity. Some dogs are trained to wear muzzles on walks to prevent them swallowing unsafe items.

442. WHY JUMP UP?

Dogs jump up to reach human faces and to gain the attention of their humans.

443. OUCH!

Jumping up is undesirable because it leads the dog to scratch and knock over unsuspecting humans!

444. TRAINING MEASURES

A dog that jumps up can be taught to sit and wait for the visitor to initiate his or her greeting.

445. DO NOT PUNISH!

Never sharply reprimand your dog for jumping up. It can teach the dog that human arrivals lead to punishment, and it can instill a fear of humans.

446. MANAGEMENT MEASURES

Installing stair gates and keeping your dog on a lead are great ways to ensure that your dog does not injure anyone while still learning to stay calm.

447. TEMPTATION EVERYWHERE
Humans are very good at leaving food and interesting items, such as shoes, for dogs to pick up and chew. This exploration is normal behavior for dogs.

448. KEEP THE FLOOR CLEAR
Especially with a puppy, leaving things lying around is an invitation to chew and ruin your items, not to mention what your dog will end up eating.

449. EATING FOOD AROUND YOUR DOG
Never share your food directly from your plate. It teaches your dog to beg from you whenever you next start eating.

450. STEALING FOOD FROM TABLES AND WORKTOPS
This can be hard to stop once your dog reaches the jackpot and steals something really tasty. Never leave your dog unsupervised while food is present.

451. RESOLVING THEFT
Always swap items for food treats, asking your dog to sit first. If your dog is persistently stealing your things, teach the thief how to bring the items to you for a reward. You'll have a very tidy house!

452. COMMUNICATION BY SOUND

Dogs communicate with a range of growls, yips, and howls, all carrying meaning. Even the humble bark can mean a number of different signals. Barks carry emotion and range widely in timing, pitch, and amplitude.

453. HOWLING

You may associate howling with wolves, but dogs can also make this quavering, drawn-out noise. Dogs howl to make contact with others, to let others know they are there, and to attract attention. They will also join in with others' howling, or in some cases, with music of a similar timbre!

454. YIPS AND YAPS

When playing or inviting another being to join in a game, dogs will often make a sharp, high-pitched yap sound. This is coupled with soft eyes and "laughing." The mouth pants, with its corners drawn back. What more of an invitation do you need to join in the fun?

455. GROWLING

A dog's growl is a low, guttural sound that is rarely mistaken. Growls are a universal signal of impending threat and danger. If your dog growls, immediately stop whatever activity is causing the stress. Growling can sometimes be playful, but is still a rehearsal of the real thing. Get expert advice on kind ways to remove related anxiety.

456. WHAT IS COMMUNICATED BY A BARK?

The duration, frequency, and pitch are important. A rapid string of high-pitched barks is a commonly recognized alarm sound, alerting others. A single bark, punctuated by pauses, often signals that the dog is alone and unhappy.

457. WHO UNDERSTANDS A BARK?

Researchers have shown that both dog owners and non-owners can identify the meanings behind barks. Each group could identify whether a bark was from a dog signaling its aloneness, its being approached by a stranger, or its playing or being aggressive.

458. DOG BARK MEANINGS FOR OTHER DOGS

We expect our dogs to understand the meaning behind other dogs' barks. During research, barks from a dog left alone did not cause listening dogs to react a great deal. However, the dogs jumped to attention when hearing a bark signaling a stranger's approach.

459. SILENCE IS GOLDEN

Barking can become a nuisance even though it is a natural behavior for dogs. "Inappropriate" or unwanted barking reflects the emotional state of the dog. It is the emotional state that must be changed, not the noise itself.

460. PREVENTING UNWANTED BARKING

If barking is undesired, list the who, what, why, where, and when of each bark for a week. This will inform you about the causes. Is it fear, loneliness, boredom, excitement, or a few of these? Help your dog to stay calm and happy in these situations, and the barking will cease.

461. CAR TROUBLE

Dogs must travel in cars in this modern world. Problems with travel can lead to serious limitations on their lives.

462. FEAR OF SOUND

Cars are noisy and vibrate as the engine roars. This can be unsettling, and the dog must learn to accept the noise by pairing it with treats.

463. MOTION SICKNESS

As a car travels around corners and over bumps in the road, as well as when starting and stopping, the movements can cause a dog to feel nauseated.

464. KEEP STILL!

As the car moves, the dog can be taught to lie down. Use a padded bed so that your dog does not roll around, too!

465. SEPARATION FROM YOU

Dogs are often expected to travel in the back of the car, but they find this distressing, as they want comfort from their owners. Aim to allow them to rest close to you if possible.

466. DRIVER SAFETY

A dog must not distract the driver in any way, so ensure your dog is not creating noise or movement that may take your attention.

467. DOG SAFETY

If your dog is loose in the car, a sudden stop or turn may cause severe injury. Keep your dog secure.

468. LEGAL SAFETY

In many countries, it is illegal to have an animal unsecured in a vehicle. Use a crate or seatbelt with a comfy protective harness.

469. GRADUAL CAR TRAINING

While your dog is still a puppy, go for short, enjoyable journeys in the car.

470. OTHER TRAFFIC

Motorcycles and other cars and trucks on the road can scare your dog or trigger the chase instinct. You can mask the view to keep your dog from being overwhelmed by what can be seen from the window.

471. MULTIPLE-DOG HOUSEHOLDS

There are complex relationships among owners and dogs in these households, and between the dogs. As a social species, dogs are inclined to seek companionship, but there also can be conflicts. Not every dog wants to live with another dog.

472. COMPATIBILITY

Ideally, dogs living in the same home are compatible and learn to live together. Hormones, possessiveness, or simply matching a young dog with an older dog can lead to problems. Each dog must have its own bed and space for undisturbed rest.

473. COMPETITION

Dogs may compete over food, toys, attention, and locations. They do not understand the concept of sharing! If one dog wants more access to these things than another one, allow it. This helps ensure the dogs do not become anxious or begin a fight over access.

474. HOME RULES

Dogs living together can learn household rules as long as the owner teaches the rules. Teach your dogs where they sleep, where they eat, and where they sit when being given food or a fuss. Rules help dogs learn how to behave calmly around one another.

475. PLACEMENT TRAINING

Teach each dog its own place in front of you. Pick, from left to right, who will sit where. This includes which dog is placed next to another. Choose the same positioning for the dogs every time you interact with them. This prevents conflict and competition for space.

476. NAMES

Use the dogs' names each time you address individuals. They will learn the sound of their own names and will learn to ignore instructions you give to other dogs. This allows you detailed control and helps the dogs to relax when their names are not mentioned.

477. PROBLEMS

Dogs may not be compatible due to hormonal clashes or the feeling that their space is overpopulated. These issues are not easy to resolve without a clinical behaviorist's assistance.

478. TO NEUTER, OR NOT?

Neutering to improve behavior around other dogs is not always the answer. Seek professional help before doing any permanent medical intervention.

479. TRAINING AND PLANNING

Training the dogs in a multiple-dog household needs to be done separately. Work with one dog and one trainer at a time. Ensure that each dog has the desired trained behavior before working on it with the dogs together. This is very important when walking the dogs on a lead.

480. START EARLY

From early puppyhood, a dog must become used to all kinds of people, especially children, in an enjoyable and fun way. Choose a puppy only from a household that can guarantee the pups were regularly played with and exposed to people from all walks of life.

481. NEW BABY

Your dog will need time to adjust to a new baby. Employ a dog walker to keep up exercise. Practice holding a doll in the same way a baby is held while your dog sits calmly. Allow your dog to sniff a baby-scented blanket before bringing the baby home.

482. KIDS

Children behave in ways that may appear
startling and unpredictable to a dog.
Teach children to behave calmly
around dogs and not to disturb them
when they are eating or resting.

483. PLAY

A dog naturally plays by mouthing, body
charging, chasing, and wrestling with other
dogs. Such games are not acceptable when
playing with people. Do not allow your dog to engage people in this
way. Likewise, prevent all humans from teaching your dog to play
rough.

484. ROUTINES

Routine is important for a pet. A human household has routines, but
a dog cannot predict what will happen during celebrations such as
fireworks or parties. Give your dog a quiet, safe place to retreat to
when routines change. Not every family dog wants to join in!

485. VISITORS

Having visitors to the home may be very exciting, or the visit may cause fearfulness and protectiveness. A dog that watches the world from front windows can quickly learn to bark at passers-by in defense. Prevent access to these areas. Teach your dog to sit calmly when visitors enter.

486. ATTENTION

Human attention is rewarding for a dog, but can reinforce unwanted behavior. People may tell a barking dog to "Be quiet." However, to the dog, this sounds like the human is joining in! Distract your barker with another activity, such as sitting, instead.

487. EMOTIONS

A dog is sensitive to the emotional atmosphere in human families. At times of stress, grieving, or arguments, your dog should be allowed to leave the room by choice. Don't be surprised if your dog's behavior changes at these times, too.

488. ATTACHMENT

A dog forms attachments that can be especially strong. This leaves the dog feeling bereft and lonely when a beloved person leaves for work or goes shopping. Teach your dog that human absence is not a problem by giving a tasty chew when you leave.

489. HOUSEHOLD RULES

Dogs do not understand human rules, and it is unfair to punish or get cross at them without setting some boundaries first. Remember, dogs LOVE routine!

490. TEAM EFFORT

Everyone who comes into contact with the dog must agree on the rules!

491. TRAINING

Some rules will need explanation. Providing easy-to-follow training, such as telling the dog to "sit" at the door before walks, means the house rules can be enforced without confusion.

492. WHO IS IN CHARGE?

It is helpful if one member of the household takes responsibility for ensuring that the house rules are followed. This is usually a responsible adult.

493. CHILDREN AND HOUSEHOLD RULES

Kids make excellent instructors as long as they know the rules. Put small signs around the house to remind them of the rules, such as the practice of making the dog sit before the dog bowl is filled.

494.
MAKE A LIST!

To make sure your rules are followed, create a roster to help the family members share tasks and timetables for training.

495. STAR CHART FOR FAMILY DOGS

Every time your dog learns a new skill, have a chart ready and add a star. You'll soon see their abilities add up!

496. "SIT" MEANS "PLEASE"

One of the best and most useful dog behaviors is sitting on command. Teach everyone that whenever your dog wants something, the rule is that the dog has to sit first, as a way to say "please."

497. RULES ARE RULES

If a member of the household refuses to follow the rules, simply prevent that person from interacting with your dog until the rules are agreed upon. Your dog will thank you for this!

498. SPEND TIME ENJOYING YOUR PET

After reading all these tips, you may feel a little overwhelmed at all the things that can or should be done. Be sure to simply spend time enjoying your dog just for being a lovely pet and companion.

499. LET DOGS BE THEMSELVES

While dogs often do things we humans don't like, you can work out what you can live with. Dogs are much happier if they can live as naturally as possible.

500. COMPANIONS TO THE LAST

We are privileged to spend our time with dogs, and they choose to be with us. Your dog will become your best friend.

501. AND FINALLY

We hope you've enjoyed this little tour through the wonderful world of dogs. Our dogs can be the most fantastic companions and our best friends in the world, but we have to live up to that promise, too. Hopefully, these tips will help make you the best friend your dog can have!

Picture Credits

Dreamstime: 9 (Wavebreakmedia), 10 (Ljupco), 11 (Dmitry Kalinovsky), 12 top (Jagodka), 24 top & 25 (Erik Lam), 37 top (Jagodka), 40 bottom (Erik Lam), 41 (One Touch Spark), 44 (Viorel Sima), 49 (Nejron), 55 (Anna Utekhina), 71 (Photodeti), 72 (Ekaterina Kurakini), 73 (Photodeti), 74 top (Nenitorx), 76 top (Odua), 77 (Monica Wizniewska), 84 (Onur Ersin), 97 top (Anke van Wyk), 100 (Jagodka), 106 (Vvs219), 106 bottom (Viorel Sima), 108 (Ivonne Wierink), 110 bottom (Jagodka), 111 (Willee Cole), 114 (Erik Lam), 116 & 120 top & 121 (Cynoclub), 120 bottom (Alexey Stiop), 122 (8213profoto), 123 (Cynoclub), 125 top (A Dog's Life Photo), 125 bottom (Alexey Kuznetsov), 127 & 133 (Erik Lam), 134 top (Stefan Hermans), 134 bottom (Andrey Yakovlev), 141 top (Andrey Popov), 141 bottom (Tyler Olson), 142 (Willee Cole), 146 & 151 bottom (Cynoclub), 152 (Farinoza), 155 bottom (Cynoclub), 158 bottom (Andrey Pavlov), 159 (Alexander Ermolaev), 166 (Sonya Etchison), 167 (Pavel Siamionau), 172 (Erik Lam), 175 bottom (Jagodka), 189 (Sergey Lavrentev), 190 (Levente Gyori), 198 top (Mila Atkovska)

Dreamstime/Eric Isselee: 7, 8, 13, 19 bottom, 22, 23 bottom, 24 bottom, 26, 27 bottom, 29 bottom, 34 bottom, 35, 36, 42, 45, 46, 47, 52, 53, 54 top, 57, 60, 64 top, 69, 78 top, 80, 92, 96, 103, 105, 109, 110 top, 119, 128–130 all, 143 top, 150, 151 top, 155 top, 185 top, 194

Fotolia: 23 top (Sparkmom), 112 (Erik Lam), 191 (Conny Hagen)

Photos.com: 17, 183

Shutterstock: 6 (Oksana Kuzmina), 12 bottom (Happy Monkey), 14 & 15 (Ann Taylor), 16 (Siamionau Pavel), 18 (Dora Zett), 19 top (Jne Valokuvaus), 20 (Elina Leonova), 21 (Dagmar Bouskova), 27 top (Rosa Jay), 28 (Dora Zett), 29 top (Kulianionak), 30 (D W Art), 31 (Alexey Kusnetsov), 32 (Csanad Kiss), 33 (Samuel Germaine-Scrivens), 34 top (Csanad Kiss), 37 bottom (Ivanova N), 38 (My Images – Micha), 39 (Cynoclub), 40 top (Pongsatom Singoy), 43 (Leoniek vander Vliet), 48 (Pardoy), 50 (Nick Chase), 51 top (Holly Cook), 51 bottom (Kateryna Shyvoronkova), 54 bottom (Susan Schmitz), 56 (Anurak Pongpatimet), 58 (Miras Wonderland), 59 (Viarel Sima), 61 (Susan Schmitz), 62 top (In

Deep), 62 bottom (Xie Wenhui), 63 (Every Dog Has A Story), 64 bottom (Ottsphoto), 65 (Studio CAXAP), 66 (Eve Photography), 67 (Andrey Kuznetsov), 68 both (Hvoya), 70 top (Nina Buday), 70 bottom (Anna Hoychuk), 74 bottom (Grigorita Ko), 75 (Nina Buday), 76 bottom (Noi 1990), 78 bottom (Billion Photos), 79 (Noi 1990), 81 (Anurak Pongpatimet), 82 (Halfpoint), 83 (Anurak Pongpatiment), 85 (Uvarov Stanislav), 86 (Adriano.cz), 87 top (135 Pixels), 87 bottom (Yakobchuk Viacheslav), 88 top (Anurak Pongpatimet), 88 bottom (Selin Aydogen), 89 (Andraskiss), 90 (Art Cook Studio), 91 top (Yellow Cat), 91 bottom (Milias 1987), 93 top (Gpointstudio), 93 bottom (Svetography), 94 (Maksimee), 95 top (Gmessina), 95 bottom (Boryana Manzurova), 97 bottom (Microstock Studio), 98 (Smit), 99 (Serghii Bobyk), 102 (Pressmaster), 104 (Kachalkina Veronika), 107 (Brian A Jackson), 113 (Vladimir Mucibabic), 115 (Nestor Rizhniak), 117 top (Billion Photos), 117 bottom (Aneta Jungerova), 118 (Reddogs), 124 (Thka), 126 (Christian Mueller), 131 (Alexei_tm), 132 (Noi 1990), 135 (Veryulissa), 136 top (Speedkingz), 136 bottom (Alexander Ermolaev), 137 (John Schulte), 138 top (Msgrafixx), 138 bottom (Cynoclub), 139 (Adriano.cz), 143 bottom (Outc), 144 (Oliver Tindall), 145 (Dora Zett), 147 (Monkey Business Images), 148 (PH888), 149 (Anucha Maneechote), 153 (Cpreiser000), 154 (Goran Cakmazovic), 156 (Romul014), 157 top (Master1305), 157 bottom (Sommart Sombutwanitkul), 158 top (Serhii Bobyk), 160 (Peter Verreussel), 161 (Gelpi), 162 (Celig), 163 (Julia Remezova), 164 (Sbko), 168 (Fotorince), 169 top (Goodluz), 169 bottom (Ovchinnikova Stanislava), 170 (Paulina Rosales), 171 (Iakov Fiulimonov), 173 (Vladimir Sukhachev), 174 (Volodymyr Burdiak), 175 top (Erik Lam), 176 (Martin Christopher Parker), 177 (Mr Nai), 178 (Dora Zett), 180 (Bormozaya), 181 top (Rarin Lee), 181 bottom (Dora Zett), 182 (Csanad Kiss), 184 (Willee Cole), 185 bottom (Robynrg), 186 (Pawel17521), 187 (Kalamurzing), 188 (Monika Wisniewska), 192 (Dora Zett), 193 (22August), 195 (Poodphoto), 196 (Meghan Huberdeau), 197 (Alexei_tm), 198 bottom (Oksana Kuzmina), 199 (Iakov Filimonov), 200 (Wavebreakmedia), 201 (Luis Molinero), 202 (Christian Mueller), 203 (Natalia Chirtsova)

Stockxpert: 140

U.S. Department of Defense: 165